THE WAY OF GOD IN THE
OLD TESTAMENT

DR. JOHN THOMAS WYLIE

authorHOUSE®

AuthorHouse™
1663 Liberty Drive
Bloomington, IN 47403
www.authorhouse.com
Phone: 1 (800) 839-8640

Published by AuthorHouse 04/06/2020

ISBN: 978-1-7283-5836-9 (sc)
ISBN: 978-1-7283-5835-2 (e)

Contents

Introduction

"How And Why"

HAVE YOU AT ANY point pondered about the world we live in? Have you at any point asked why things are how they are? There are numerous things about our reality that cause us to ask "How?" and "why?" - things that individuals have been getting some information about since the get-go.

Antiquated individuals used to wonder, "For what reason do the seasons go back and forth? For what reason do leaves burst from their buds in the springtime? For what reason do they change shading in the fall? For what reason do they die and drop to make the progress in winter?"

Numerous things like this never again bewilder us. We have realized why the seasons come and go. We know how our earth circles around the sun, tilted only a little on its axis; in summer we are warmed more by the sun's beams than in winter.

Today we see substantially more about things that occur in our general surroundings. Be that as it may, regardless we wonder, as people did quite a while in the past, at life itself, at all the living things around us, and at our very own being alive. About this marvel of life, regardless we ask, "how?" and "why?"

Chapter One

Answers From Long Ago

THE HEBREW PEOPLE WHO lived some time in the past ages articulate what they accepted about the wonder of the world and of all the life in it. We read their words in the beginning of the Bible. These words express the solid sentiments of wonder and wonderment that people wherever have when they contemplate things that are significant however difficult to get it.

What they composed just says, "God made the world with every one of its marvels and all its superb ways; and God needed it to be a good world." These words state in a fine way what Christian people of today believe too.

Genesis 1:1-24a. Two thoughts are rehashed again and again in the story. They reveal to us the huge facts that the story needs us to know. Look in these verses in chapter 1 to find them: 3 and 4a; 9 and 10b; 11 and 12b; 14-15 and 18b; 24 and 25b; 26 and 31a. (The letter "a" after the number for a verse means the first part of the verse; "b" means the second part, etc.) These two sentences recount to the whole story: 1:1 and 1:31a.

"Genesis" is a good title for the book of the Bible where this story is composed (written). "Genesis" is a Greek word which means "beginnings."

But Why Is There Wrong In The World?

Sometimes answers only bring up more questions! The men of quite a while in the past wrote in Genesis that God made the world to be good. Be that as it may, when they glanced around at the world where they lived, they saw something different. What they saw caused them to ask, "For what reason is there wrong in God's world?"

As we check out the present world, we wonder something very similar. We see that not everything about the world is good. A great deal of things are out and out terrible! Young men and young ladies have battles on the play area; grown-ups have their contentions; countries do battle. Most likely something isn't right when people battle and damage and execute each other.

It is plain to see that a ton isn't right in this world that God made and intended to be a good world. It is anything but difficult to perceive any reason why people quite a while in the past (the ancients) thought about how this could be.

Another Answer To A Question We Ask

The essayist of Genesis responded to this inquiry in another story. It is straightforward enough for everybody to get it. This story is around two individuals, Adam and Eve. Be that as it may, their names could have been "You" and "I," for the story about this man and this woman is our story, as well.

Is anything but an account of something that happened once in a time in the past yesterday; it is the narrative of what continues happening today-and again tomorrow.

Genesis 3. Do we know what God wants us to do? Do we know when we accomplish something God doesn't want us to do? What makes a thing wrong? For what reason do we foul up things? What is our opinion about the inappropriate things we do? Verses

2b-3, 6, and 8 recount to this story in only a few words.

A Story About Us

Do you start to perceive what the issue is? Do you start to perceive any reason why the world God wants for us never fully works out as expected? God didn't put manikins on his earth.

Manikins consistently would make the best decision, for God would be "pulling the strings." he would do all their reasoning and choosing for them. Rather, God made people with a through and through freedom (free will) to settle on decisions.

He made these people- us-in his own image. That is, from multiple points of view we are something like God himself. He has enabled us to pass judgment and choose. He has enabled us to choose among good and bad, among great and abhorrence, among obeying and disobeying, between accomplishing things his way or our own particular way. This make us the people that we are.

In any case, how would we use this power God has given us? It is safe to say that we are obedient or rebellious to God who made us? The narrative of Adam and Eve disclose to us what we do. Despite the fact that we know we should

Dr. John Thomas Wylie

obey God, we want to work for ourselves. We want to run our very own lives to suit ourselves as opposed to obeying God's ways for us. People consistently have been like this.

The consequence of this is plain to see. At the point when we decide to do what we want as opposed to doing what we know God wants, we ruin everything God meant for us. The wrong in us makes the world the manner in which it is rather than the manner in which God proposed it to be.

Be that as it may, to top it all off, a wrong in us means that we don't believe God as he wants us to. Our word for this, for this unsoundness in us, is "sin." Therefore, we as a whole are sinners.

Chapter Two

The Fathers Of A People

"LONG, LONG AGO IN the past and far away...." This is how many of our preferred stories begin. This is the means by which the way of God in the Old Testament begins, as well. It takes us back thousands of years to the opposite side of the earth to a land called the "Fertile Crescent."

This Fertile Crescent is a half circle of once green land that curves up over and around the Arabian Desert. One tip of it contacts the Persian Gulf in the east. From that point it spreads up and westbound until it bends down again along the Mediterranean Sea. Its western tip comes to on toward the south. There it approaches the mouth of the Nile River in Egypt.

For thousands of years before Bible times, people had moved into the Fertile Crescent to live. A portion of these were likely the first people in all the world to settle down to live as farmers.

They most likely were the first people to build urban areas (cities) to live in. A spot in the eastern part of the Fertile Crescent would have been the best place in all the ancient world for that. Here was a rich, flood-washed plain between two incredible rivers, the Tigris and the Euphrates.

This was the land that consistently has been called Mesopotamia. The name is perfect for it; Mesopotamia signifies "between the rivers." Here, some place "between the rivers," lived the people whom God used to begin showing himself to us.

A Man Called Abraham

Our story truly begins with a man - and close to a bustling city in eastern Mesopotamia. The man was a shepherd called Abram. The Bible later talks about him as "Abraham," so that is the name that we will call him in our story. The city was called Ur of the Chaldeans.

Chaldea was a name the Bible authors used for Babylonia, one of the ancient countries of Mesopotamia. The time most likely was around 1750 B.C. or then again maybe it was 200 years before that. We only realize that during those years huge quantities of meandering shepherds like Abraham climbed from the desert into the

Fertile Crescent and afterward westbound toward Canaan.

Since we don't know precisely when Abraham lived, you may have speculated that there are different parts of his anecdote about which we know just a little or nothing. An incredible narrative was not explicitly put in writing at the time.

There was a valid justification for this. Abraham and his relatives didn't try to figure out how to peruse and compose. They recounted to their accounts again and again from age to age. Just the copyists (scribes) of city people set aside some effort to record whatever could be told simply.

Abraham's story more likely than not been imperative to his relatives, however. A few hundred years after the fact, when they had settled down to live in urban areas, they composed two long stories about him and his family.

In these accounts they disclose to us how this Abraham, a meandering shepherd, turned into the "father of a new nation of people - their very own Hebrew country. What's more, they disclose to us how these people came to live in their own land, Canaan. "Our God wanted this for Abraham and for us," they state in their accounts again and again.

Two Stories About Abraham

The first story about Abraham and his relatives was composed by Hebrews who lived in the southern part of Canaan. It generally discusses the Hebrews' God by a name, "Yahweh." In that day every one of the people of the Fertile Crescent called every god by a name-similarly as every person was called by his very own name.

In our Bible this Hebrew name Yahweh is composed either "Jehovah" or "Lord." In our story we will say "Jehovah" since this sounds most like a genuine name. "How might we address our God or request that he help us if we didn't have a clue about his name?" the ancient Hebrews would state to us. They were certain that Jehovah consistently listened when they spoke his name.

The second story about Abraham and his relatives was composed a lot later by Hebrews who lived in the northern part of Canaan. It uses a word that other people of Canaan used when they discussed their divine beings (gods).

This word, "Elohim, was their method for

Dr. John Thomas Wylie

saying "most noteworthy god." (Every nation, obviously, was certain that its own god was the "greatest god" of all!). Despite the fact that this word doesn't mean precisely what we mean when we state "God," in our Bible Elohim is expressed "God."

It appears to be bizarre to us that these accounts don't talk about God precisely as we do today, however there is a valid justification why they proved unable. You know now what this explanation was. In that day, everybody in the Fertile Crescent accepted that there were many, numerous divine beings (gods). Nobody had come to know yet that there is only one, true God.

Various divine beings lived and managed in various lands, they accepted. They were certain that there were various divine beings for a wide range of powers in nature and that there were various divine beings for various countries and for various clans of people, as well.

No big surprise they called every god by his own name! "How might you approach the right god for help in the event that you didn't have the foggiest idea about his name?" they would say to us. They were certain that these divine beings tuned in to them when they addressed them.

Many, numerous years after both these accounts had been composed, still other obscure authors wove them together into one story. This account of the Hebrew ancestors is the story we have in our Bible today. As we read it, we know the awesome truth that the Hebrews still needed to learn.

One day they would come to realize that Jehovah, their Elohim, genuinely was God, the true God of all the earth. So when they recount to us in their accounts how Jehovah addressed them, we know that God truly was addressing them-and to us, as well.

Traditions From The Past

It is straightforward that a lot of Abraham's story probably been lost before anything was expounded on him. To comprehend that numerous stories about him more likely than not grown up during those hundreds of years. Maybe that is the reason Abraham's relatives frequently had various thoughts regarding who he truly was.

"A meandering Aramean was my father," a portion of the Hebrews said of Abraham. (Deu. 26:5).

"Your dad was an Amorite, and your mom a Hittite," different Hebrews reminded them." (Ezekiel 16:3, 45)

What a mistake in the family tree! In any case, they all more likely than not concurred when they were told, "Your fathers lived of old past the Euphrates...and they served different divine beings." (Joshua 24:2).

Everybody realized that every one of these human Arameans, Amorites, and Hittites- once had lived in far away lands. What's more, obviously, they all had venerated the many, numerous divine forces of their old lands.

In any case, presently, what did it make a difference who Abraham's ancestors were or what divine beings they had loved and worshiped? Their story, the Hebrews' story, started with Abraham.

That was when Jehovah became his God and theirs. Their great-great-great-great grandparents didn't make a difference. Abraham was their "father" and Jehovah was their God. Each Hebrew knew that.

Maybe other people who lived in the Fertile Crescent at that point have revealed to us something about Abraham's relatives may have overlooked or even may never have known these things. Archeologists have discovered clay tablets from this period that talk about the 'Apiru or Habiru, a word signifying "wanderers."

Researchers accept that this word in the long run became "Ibris or Hebrews. Obviously, every "vagabond" couldn't have been a Hebrew. In any case, each Hebrew was certain that the Habiru or "wanderer" Abraham was his ancestor.

Every one of these things give us why we can't make certain about a significant number of the subtleties of Abraham's story as we have it now. In any case, we are certain that it discloses to us what ages of Hebrew storytellers and scholars knew was significant about it.

They were certain that Jehovah had wanted their progenitors to know him and to serve and obey him. That is the extremely significant thing for us, as well. That was the means by which God began to show himself to them and us.

So now, back again to Ur of the Chaldeans and the beginning of our story.

Ur Of The Chaldeans

We know since Ur was an extraordinary city of the old world in Abraham's day. Maybe a fourth of a million people lived inside its solid, safe walls. Experts worked in the shops that lined its restricted lanes.

Early consistently farmers went out to care for the grain fields and gardens and palm forests around the city. Engineers were grinding away building and fixing the channels that conveyed water from the Euphrates to irrigate these rich fields.

Mariners and dockworkers were occupied at Ur's harbor, as well, for then the Persian Gulf came exceptionally near this incredible city.

The first sight to welcome explorers coming to Ur via land or via ocean would have been the glimmering temple at the very top of the city's monster ziggurat. Ur's incredible ziggurat, a man-made pile of earth and block, transcend over the city's mud-brick houses and walls.

From his temple high on this ziggurat, Ur's moon god Sin looked downward on the city and out of sight the encompassing open country. Their moon god Sin deserved such a fine temple, everybody in Ur was certain. Season after season he reliably brought the downpours and the floods that watered their rich land. Ur was grateful for Sin's consideration.

Did youthful Abraham ever observe this popular milestone from far, far away? Did he ever leave his flocks to pursue seeing it until he came into the city itself? Did he ever move up its several stairs, carrying a sacrifice to provide for the moon god, Sin?

Did he go into other temples to solicit the assistance from Shamash, the sun god, or to go to Ishtar, the goddess of war? Did he ever wonder which divine force (which god) of all the numerous gods of the land must be the most dominant?

We will never know the responses to these inquiries, for this would have happened just before our story starts.

Journey To A New Land

After Abraham had developed to masculinity and married, his father Terah chose to move to Canaan with his family.

Maybe field land was getting rare close to Ur. Or then again maybe the family had gotten fretful and was searching for experience. Whatever the explanation, they left Ur and started the moderate voyage toward Canaan.

It was difficult to move a huge family and its flocks starting with one spot then onto the next. There would be peril up and down the way. What's more, when the explorers landed in another nation, how might they be invited? Assume the people or the gods of the place were not cordial? It was a dangerous business!

Maybe these questions kept Terah from taking his family right to Canaan. At any rate, when the explorers landed at Haran, they remained there. Maybe it was ideal to settle there where different drifters (wanderers) such as themselves had come to live.

On To Canaan

When Terah passed on, Abraham turned into the leader of the growing group. At that point the family moved once more. In any case, this time, we are told, they moved due to a unique explanation.

Genesis 12:1-3. These verses reveal to us what the Hebrew story writers were certain Jehovah wanted for Abraham-and his relatives. What was it?

How could Abraham at any point become the

father of a whole country of people? This elderly person and his significant other didn't have a child to bury them when they passed on. Furthermore, for what reason would it be a good idea for them to go to Canaan? There doubtlessly should be other people living there.

By and by, Abraham confided in Jehovah, our story lets us know. He was certain that Jehovah wanted him to go to Canaan. In this way, by and by, the drifters (wanderers) set off. Abraham was becoming old. Would he have the option to direct and deal with an enormous convoy as they ventured along the unpleasant trails to Canaan? When voyagers arrived at Damascus, maybe nobody would mind to proceed.

Be that as it may, go on they did! Abraham and his family kept endlessly toward the south. At last they arrived at Canaan.

After several years, Abraham's relatives were certain this had arranged the path for them to live in Canaan. (see Genesis 12:4-6) This was the land that Jehovah unquestionably consistently had wanted them to call their own-the "Promised Land."

Genesis 12:7. This verse discloses to us what the Hebrews were certain Jehovah wanted for

Abraham and for them. For what reason did the Hebrews come to consider Canaan the "Promised Land?"

Stories With Surprise Endings

What did the Canaanites think about this invasion? Fortunately for Abraham, they were use to wanderers who traveled every which way, after quite a long time after year. At that point, as well, these newcomers were serene. Things were getting somewhat swarmed, however, particularly when the downpours fizzled and the grass died.

Abraham's people had brought along extraordinary groups of sheep that required water and great green fields. Also, presently, water openings were evaporating. The fields got dry. Before long the individuals themselves would be ravenous.

The Canaanites likely were happy when Abraham and his huge family moved south again looking for better fields and water. It generally had been similar to this with these wandering shepherds. In the midst of dry season or starvation (famine) they would proceed onward to locate a superior home. They may even go right to Egypt.

There the land consistently was watered by the Nile.

As the story tells it, Abraham went to Egypt. Is it accurate to say that he was overlooking that Jehovah needed him to live in Canaan? Is it true that he was leaving Canaan, never to returned again? (See Genesis 12:10).

Hundreds of years after the fact, Hebrew members more likely than not moaned in help (see Genesis 13:1) when the story teller proceeded to state, "Yet Jehovah brought our father Abraham up from Egypt to Canaan once more."

A Dangerous Chance

Home once more! That is the manner by which Abraham more likely than not felt as he approached Canaan. Be that as it may, when the clan got to the ripe inclines of the mountains once more, the quietness of the days of yore was absent. Presently there was quarreling among the shepherds about the best field or water opening.

It was chosen that Lot, Abraham's nephew, and his family and supporters should leave Abraham. Parcel ought to pick the land wherein he wanted to live. Would Lot want the land that was intended to have a place with Abraham and his relatives?

It appeared that each time Abraham was prepared to settle in this Promised Land, something happened to forestall it. To begin with, starvation had removed him from it and driven him into Egypt; presently, this!

As it turned out, Lot chose the prolific plain of the Jordan, leaving the mountains of Canaan to Abraham. Abraham's relatives were certain this was only the manner in which Jehovah had wanted things to show up for Abraham-and for them.

Laughter At Last

Abraham and Sarah, rich as they were, still couldn't be happy. As the years passed, their misery developed. More than everything else on the planet, they wanted their very own child. Abraham truly had one child now, but this kid, Ishmael, was the child of his slave spouse, Hagar.

That made Ishmael a slave, as well. Abraham needed Sarah to have a child who might turn into the following head (leader) of their family or clan. Without this child, Abraham never could turn into the father of a great nation. Could Jehovah truly have wanted that for him?

Abraham's relatives, tuning in to his story, more likely than not held their breath holding back to hear what occurred straightaway. The appropriate response that they knew so all around appeared to be another supernatural occurrence (a miracle) each time they heard it told over once more. A child was destined to Abraham and Sarah. The name they gave the youngster recounted their joy; Isaac signifies "he laughs." Surely Jehovah had given them this child. Now Abraham could be the father of a great many ages of people who might live in the Promised Land.

Strange Stories Of Strange Ways

After this we hear a few stories that the Hebrews wanted to tell again and again. These appear to be weird and barbarous to us-until we find what they were intended to tell.

One of these accounts tells how Abraham's slave spouse and her little child were driven from the clan since Abraham and Sarah had their very own child. The woman and her youngster were carried into the desert alone amazing! What a merciless thing!

Such a dreadful thing could have occurred in that day, obviously, however this story was told for an alternate reason. It was another way the Hebrews told their children how sure they were that Jehovah consistently had wanted them-rather than other "wanderers" like them-to live in Canaan to serve him.

The Hebrew's called themselves "Isaac's children." They thought of these other "wanderers" who lived in the desert as their far off family members (distant relatives), "the offspring of Ishmael." So this story truly clarified how these people who were a lot of the same came to live in various lands. The Hebrews were certain that Jehovah had wanted it to be as such.

Another weird story makes us wonder how Isaac ever could have relatives to serve Jehovah in Canaan. Abraham was going to sacrifice Isaac to Jehovah! He was certain that Jehovah wanted him to do this.

What a horrendous thing! In any case, we know that many people of that day accepted, and believed that a man's first child ought to be yielded to their horrible divine beings. We are happy that this story ended all the more cheerfully. Since Abraham would have obeyed, the story says, Isaac was to live to become the following father of the Hebrew people all things considered.

Maybe this story also told the Hebrews that Jehovah didn't want them to sacrifice their children to him. We trust it did. In any case, as our story goes on, we will perceive how regularly regardless they expected to discover that! Sometime in the not so distant future, however, maybe they would adapt better approaches to serve God.

Isaac Becomes The Chieftain

We don't peruse substantially more about Isaac until the opportunity arrived for him to be given a spouse. At that point, in a long story, our writers disclose to us how Abraham sent a worker (servant) to the Hebrews' family members near Haran to discover a spouse for Isaac.

Near Haran, where the Hebrews family members lived, the worker found precisely the right spouse for Isaac. Her name was Rebekah. Our story scholars were certain that Jehovah wanted the worker (servant) to choose this young woman who went to the well and drew water for his parched "camels." They reveal to us that Rebekah's family, as well, was certain that Jehovah wanted her to be Isaac's better half. (Beginning 24)

Now Isaac was prepared to be the next chief of the clan. Doubtlessly he would have children of his own to follow him. So now our story discloses to us the most significant thing of about him.

Genesis 26:1-5. Prior in their story, the scholars were certain Jehovah had wanted these things for another person. Who was it?

After this we don't find considerably more about Isaac until his twin children were conceived. At that point we discover that he didn't care for Jacob as much as he preferred the other twin, Esau.

At the point when we initially meet him, we, as well, think that its difficult to like Jacob whose name signifies "cheater."(25:19-34) Yet, it was this cheater who became the next ancestor (forefather) of the Hebrew people. How could this be?

Jacob The Cheater

Jacob and Esau must have fought with one another from youth. They generally would be rivals, however just one of them could be the victor. Uncalled for as it might appear, it generally was Jacob who proved to be the best.

Jacob misled (trick, deceived) his old father Isaac into giving him the "blessing" or legacy (inheritance) that Isaac thought he was promising to Esau. This was not kidding. When it was given, a withering man's blessing couldn't be reclaimed. Whatever he said "must be"-regardless of whether he committed an error or not.

Thus, by guile, Jacob was to become the new chieftain of the family. He would be a ground-breaking, well off man when Isaac passed on. Esau would need to be a wandering desert migrant (a nomad). (Genesis 27:1-40)

Run, Jacob, Run

Esau couldn't overlook that this riches and influence should been promised to him. He was the "first-born" of Isaac's twin children. In his resentment, he thought of an arrangement for settling the score. Be that as it may, Rebekah learned of Easu's plot; she immediately convinced Isaac to send Jacob away-to look for a spouse.

What a cunning way this was to get Jacob securely out of Esau's range!

Jacob readily began toward Haran in Paddan-aram. In transit, however, something strange happened to this startled, fleeing cheater. Our story writers inform us concerning it in their account of Jacob's peculiar, but strange dream.

Genesis 28:10-18. People of the ancient world believed that their gods often spoke to them through dreams. This reveals to us what the Hebrews were certain Jehovah had wanted for Jacob and for them. Did they believed that Jehovah had wanted good things for Esau and his relatives, as well? Did they need to learn that God wants good things for everyone?

When Jacob arose from this strange dream, he vowed to trust in Jehovah if Jehovah would take care of him. This appears to us to be an extremely abnormal sort of a can hope for a man to make with God. Simply envision somebody disclosing to God what he should do before he will be faithful to him!

That was the route people of the ancient world thought of their divine beings (gods), however, so this didn't appear to be unusual to our story writers.

How could a man like Jacob at any point become a part of God's way for carrying the world's people to think about him? One day Isaac would die. Jacob, the con artist, would take his place. What might happen at that point?

On The Run Again

When Jacob got to Haran, he settled down to can anticipate a spouse from among his family members. There the tables were turned for once. Jacob himself was deceived. He was given Leah for a lady of the hour (wife) rather than the beautiful Rachel whom he wanted.

Be that as it may, it didn't make a difference. He did what he generally did when there was something he truly wanted. He kept right on laboring for seven additional years to win Rachel from Laban, her insightful father. After that the ball was in Jacob's court to swindle Laban by promising the best animals of Laban's flocks for his wages.

With two spouses, two other slave wives, and a few tents loaded with youngsters, Jacob was a well off man when he had tricked Laban out of the entirety of his riches. By then, he realized he would be wise to escape the country (Genesis

31:1-3)- despite the fact that that implied returning to Canaan and taking his risks with Esau.

Laban's understanding with his son- in-law had worn to a fatigue. Pretty much all the poor man had left was his family's idols. In any case, they were his most esteemed belongings. The child to whom he gave them would be the following leader of the family.

While Laban and his son's were away shearing the couple of hopeless sheep Jacob had left them, Jacob and his huge family furtively stole away to go to Canaan. With them they took a large portion of Laban's flocks and his divine beings (idol gods). Rebekah had taken in Jacob's stunts; she had taken Laban's idols similarly as Jacob had taken his brother's legacy. This time, however, Jacob was guiltless.

After seven years it appeared that Jacob's flawless arrangement had fizzled and that Rebekah's burglary would cost her life. That was when Laban got up to speed with his escaping son-in-law and daughters. Be that as it may, once more, the cheaters there were two of them now- pulled off their tricks. Laban returned to Haran as with practically nothing as he had come (Genesis 31:22-55).

Jacob Becomes "Israel"

After Laban had returned toward Haran, Jacob wanted to begin pondering his other issue Esau. Meeting his irate sibling terrified him nearly to death. Jacob was certain that now he was going to get precisely what he deserved.

That became completely clear when he discovered that Easu was coming to meet him-with 400 outfitted tribesmen at his heels. The con artist (Jacob) was in for it. It is difficult to comprehend why he never had been gotten.

It is much harder to comprehend why our authors were certain that Jehovah had helped Jacob this time. They were certain that Jehovah had wanted Jacob to take Esau's legacy. They were certain that Jehovah had wanted Jacob to have all Laban's riches. They were certain that Jehovah had wanted Jacob to escape from Haran and to return to Canaan securely. How could that be?

To our essayists, the appropriate response was straightforward: Jehovah had helped Jacob with the goal that they, his relatives, could become a country in Canaan. Since Jacob was to be the following progenitor of these people, we are happy to find what occurred straightaway.

Genesis 32:9-12. How has Jacob transformed from the sort of person he was previously?

After his prayer, a grieved, humble Jacob sent a parade of

endowments on in front of him to Esau. He truly had changed! Our writers' next story about Jacob reveals to us that finally he even came to trust in Jehovah.

Genesis 32:22-30. People of the ancient world believed that their divine beings (gods) may come to them as "men" or "angels." The ancient Hebrews accepted this, as well.

Now, Jacob, the man who had changed his ways, would be called by his changed name, as well. The new name, "Israel" may have signified "God strives" or "God never gives up." That was a good name for Jacob. God never had quit any pretense of wanting him to change.

After this, we are happy that Esau didn't hurt Jacob and his family. What's more, we are happy to hear what our scholars let us know straightaway. (Genesis 35:9-15). Jacob, the man who changed, truly was to be the father of the nation of people who might live in Canaan.

Many years after the fact when Jacob died on in Egypt, he had the adoration of his children and the respect of his people. In any case, how as it that he spent his old age in Egypt? Did he desert the Promised Land all things considered? What were Jacob and his people doing so far away from their own nation?

The Hard Road To Egypt

The story of Jacob came to be in Egypt truly starts with the account of his preferred (favorite) son, Joseph. What's more, that story starts on the day that Jacob's ten most established children came to him with unfortunate news. Joseph, they let him know, had been executed by wild creatures.

They had only his long coat with sleeves to show Jacob. It was all blood-stained and torn. Jacob's preferred (favorite) son unquestionably was dead.

Jacob consistently had known that his more seasoned children didn't understand Joseph and his ways. They had considered him a busybody, a braggart, and a visionary (dreamer) who thought he was superior to his brothers. In any case, Jacob never presumed what truly had occurred (Genesis 37).

After that heart break, a dry spell (famine) struck Canaan once more, similarly as it had in the time of Abraham. After the first year, the dry spell (famine) brought starvation; the starvation would bring death. There was only one expectation. Jacob's people must get nourishment (food) from Egypt. In spite of the fact that the dry season had arrived at Egypt, as well, there still was nourishment (food) there. This was all a direct result of one man, our author lets us know. His name, obviously, was Joseph (Genesis 39-41)!

Joseph In Egypt

Joseph was not dead. He had not been murdered. His siblings had offered him to merchants (traders) who had accepted him to Egypt as a slave. As he was exchanged starting with one master then onto the next, however, his fortune had gotten better and better. At long last, he had come to be a person from the Pharaoh's very own family unit.

Actually, it was Joseph who had advised the Pharaoh to store away grain when it was copious, our story lets us know. He was certain that it before long would be required. So for a long time the Pharaoh's storage facilities had been filled until they could hold no more. At that point the starvation came. No big surprise Joseph now was the Grand Vizier of Egypt, next in power to the Pharaoh himself (Genesis 41).

Back in Canaan Jacob chose that his children ought to go to Egypt to bring back grain. Every one of the siblings would go aside from Joseph's more youthful brother, Benjamin. This was the son whom Jacob loved now as he once had loved Joseph.

Consider the possibility that the ten siblings had known that the man in Egypt from whom they asked grain was Joseph. They were scared enough as it seemed to be! That they were so happy to escape from this bizarre land and to be back home once more (Genesis 42)).

Be that as it may, soon the nourishment (food) was no more. Every one of the brothers went to Egypt for nourishment once more; this was the moment for which Joseph had deliberately planned. Their secret, and his, was out (Genesis 43-44).

Genesis 45:1-15. These verses determine what happened when Joseph told his siblings what his identity was. The Hebrew scholars were certain that Jehovah had wanted Joseph to spare his kin. What words reveal to you this?

The Pharaoh was happy to have Joseph's family come to Egypt, despite the fact that they were shepherds. He even gave them rich farmland in Goshen for a home (Genesis 47:1-12).

Jacob's People In Egypt

When the time arrived for Jacob to die he called his children around him to give them his blessing. Twelve children! What's more, when Abraham, their great-grandfather, had surrendered any desire for having any family to remember him! Would these twelve children of Jacob ever discover their way back to the Promised Land?

Would their relatives ever live in their very own territory and become a country? (49:1-27). When Jacob last spoke to his children (his sons), he asked that his body be taken to the land that is known for his ancestors (the land of his forefathers). There it was to lie next to his forefathers. Abraham and Sarah, and Issac and Rebekah, in a cave in a field in Canaan (49:29-32).

To what extent would it be before Jacob's people would returned to Canaan, as well? Furthermore, to what extent would it be before they would be a country that could show God to his world?

Chapter Three

The Great Rescue

To WHAT EXTENT WOULD it be before the Hebrews left Egypt to come back to the land they called home?

Their stay in Egypt this time was not a short one as it had been for Abraham. Truth be told, it more likely than not kept going in excess of 400 years. What might Jacob have thought if he could have known that his great-great-great- great-great grand-children still would live where he had come uniquely to get away from the horrible starvation in Canaan?

Treasure Cities And Troubles

Jacob never could have thought about what might occur for his people during every one of those years. In the event that he could have known, he doubtlessly would have kept his family in Canaan to die of starvation there. The Hebrews were in a tough situation now. They were in a difficult situation.

When the Hebrews initially came to Egypt, they had been welcome visitors of the Pharaoh. Now they were his detainees (slaves). At that point they had been given rich grazing area for their herds.

Now they couldn't consider their lives their own. At that point they had wondered about Egypt's awesome sanctuaries (temples) and goliath pyramid tombs; slaves had fabricated these for the pharaohs several years prior. Now the Hebrews were slaves, making bricks for another pharaoh's new "treasure urban communities" at the mouth of the Nile. What was the deal? Maybe it was this.

When Egypt's Rulers Changed

Egypt consistently was being attacked by people who needed its wealth, its nourishment, its valuable metals. At some point before the times of Joseph, people called the Hyksos had attacked the land. Rather than leaving with their plunder, however, these people had stayed-and had become Egypt's rulers.

Dr. John Thomas Wylie

These Hyksos were people much like the Hebrews. This would clarify why a man like Joseph could have ascended to a high position and why his family would have found a cordial greeting in Egypt. The Hyksos probably been ruling Egypt at that point.

It took the Egyptians around one hundred and forty years to dispose of the Hyksos. Maybe a considerable lot of the Hebrews were driven from Egypt alongside them. The individuals who were left more likely than not been subjugated and set to work for the new pharaohs. Now, as another part of our story begins, life for these Hebrews in Egypt was deteriorating and more regrettable.

The Egyptians dreaded this growing group of outsiders. On the off chance that different intruders like the Hyksos should come thumping on Egypt's entryways, these Hebrews very well might attempt to assist them with getting in! The best activity, the Egyptians had chosen, was to dispose of these slaves.

The physically fit men were to be worked to death; male youngsters were not to be allowed to grow up. That would deal with them. (Exodus

1:8-22). Be that as it may, it didn't. The Hebrew family in Egypt only became larger and larger.

Moses Comes On The Scene

It would have been hard around then to perceive how these people ever could assist God with revealing himself to the world. Thinking back on what occurred straightaway, however, we can see that at this very point God was starting to use them for that.

A man-one Hebrew man-came to realize that Jehovah wanted to safeguard these people. His name was Moses. This Moses was to become the most notable person in all of Hebrew history. It is no big surprise that numerous stories about him grew up to be told and retold by the Hebrews similarly as stories about their forefathers grew up to be told again and again (Exodus 2:1-10).

In the most established story about Moses that came to be written in our Bible, we meet him one day as he was watching his sibling Hebrews at their backbreaking work. In an eruption of outrage, Moses killed an Egyptian taskmaster who was abusing one of the Hebrews slaves. Therefore, he became a criminal, a fugitive (Exodus 2:11-20).

Where could Moses go to hide to escape from the Pharaoh's officials? He pursued a caravan course that carried him to the place that is known for the wandering Midianites. There, among these people, he carried on with the life of a shepherd.

At that point our story discloses to us how in this tough and rugged land, at the foot of an infertile, three-topped mountain, Moses came to find out about Jehovah. Simultaneously he came to comprehend what Jehovah wanted him to do.

(Exodus 3:1-15). What did Moses come to realize he should do? Verses 13-15 disclose to us that the Hebrews would need to discover that Jehovah was the God of their forefathers. In the greater part of the Hebrews' accounts, Mount Horeb is called Mount Sinai.

The Hard Task

Moses didn't accept that he could enable the Hebrews to escape from Egypt. Following 400 years the Hebrews didn't remember any god of their forefathers! They didn't have a clue what Jehovah's identity was! If Moses revealed to them what Jehovah wanted for them, they wouldn't trust him.

This task called for somebody who could convince the Hebrews that Jehovah was genuine and that he truly thought about them. Moses was certain he never could do this! No big surprise he started to consider pardons for not taking on such a troublesome undertaking.

In any case, what Jehovah wanted was clear. The Hebrew people were to leave Egypt; Moses was to lead them to Canaan. Numerous things would hinder them but Moses, with Jehovah's assistance, would beat them all.

Moses at long last realized he should do what he was certain Jehovah wanted him to do. Finally he told the people that their forgotten God Jehovah would assist them with getting away from Egypt. Incredibly, they trusted him! In any case, what chance was there that the Pharaoh would release them (Exodus 4:29-31)?

The future looked dark to be sure when Moses addressed the Pharaoh. The ruler's answer was a flat "No!" Worse yet, he demanded that the Hebrews slaves work more diligently (harder) than at any other time. No big surprise the Hebrews quit trusting Moses and his wild thoughts at that point! it was practically enough to make Moses himself quit believing (Exodus 5:1-23).

In any case, that was not the end of the issue. Jehovah continued disclosing to Moses that the Hebrews must return to Canaan. At last, with the assistance of his brother Aaron, Moses got Pharaoh to give the Hebrews a chance to leave Egypt. in a long story made up of numerous accounts which the Hebrews told again and again, we read of horrendous things that happened to the Egyptians.

These stories about "plagues" reveal to us how sure the Hebrews were that Jehovah had helped them escape from Egypt. The Hebrews were certain that Jehovah had been more dominant than the Pharaoh and every one of the divine forces (gods) of Egypt. They were certain that Jehovah had wanted them to go to Canaan; they were certain Jehovah had helped them (Exodus 7:1-12:39).

Get Away From Egypt

Did the Hebrews know precisely where Canaan was? Did they realize that huge numbers of their family members must live there? We don't have the foggiest idea. In any case, we do realize that it took mental fortitude and confidence for them to strike out for this new land. They would have no maps, no compasses; there would be no street signs or even streets as we probably am aware them.

Long periods of living in a ripe, green land had not readied the Hebrews for the desolate, waterless extends through which they would need to travel.

Today we can't make certain of the course that Moses and his people pursued. Huge numbers of the spots referenced in the Exodus story can't be found at this point. Some have been cleared out by changes in the geography of the land. The Bible story discloses to us that they did not go to the place where there is the Philistines.

This would have been the briefest way, however it was a fundamental procession and military course thus it was watched by Egyptian soldiers. They certainly couldn't go out and about. Rather, the Hebrews went on an indirect adventure from Rameses to Etham, a spot on the edge of the wilderness.

Leaving Ethan, they backtracked to what the Bible calls the "Red Sea." Bible researchers presently consider this the "Reed Sea" or the "Sea of Reeds," for it was not the Red Sea we know today. It was tight, shallow, reed-stifled swamp at the highest point of the Gulf of Suez (Exodus 13:17,18).

Saved

Just as the escaping Hebrews came to the present circumstance of marshy Sea of Reeds (Red Sea), they located a column of Egyptian chariots hunkering down on them. Regardless of everything that had happened to him and his people on account of these Hebrew slaves and their God, the Pharaoh had concluded that he couldn't bear to lose every one of these laborers all things considered.

What occurred next was to be the most significant occasion in every one of the Hebrews history.

Exodus 14:5-31; 15:19-21. This is the Hebrews' account of their break through the Red Sea (Sea of Reeds). Exodus 15:21 is a renowned triumph melody; it is probably the most seasoned verse in the Bible.

What had happened was a miracle, the Hebrews were certain. Envision! They had been brought securely to the opposite side of the Sea of Reeds (Red Sea). The Egyptian officers in their chariots had been caught in its swamp and waters.

Saved! Saved! "This is the thing that Jehovah has accomplished for us," the Hebrews cried. "This is the thing that Jehovah accomplished for our fathers when we were slaves in Egypt," their children would remember through every one of the hundreds of years to come.

At Jehovah's Mountain

Canaan still was far off, however. Could the Hebrews endure the desert venture that currently lay before them?

They survived! At the point when things looked blackest, they were given water to drink and nourishment to eat, or they were outwitted their desert foes. (Exodus 15:22-25a; 16:1-21). At the point when these beneficial things occurred, they generally made certain to cry, "Jehovah has done this to us." But at that point, in the following breath, they would protest about some hardship.

With their backs to Egypt, the Hebrew people turned south on the Sinai Peninsula. They presumably pursued a course which had been used for quite a long time by laborers heading off to the rich copper and turquoise mines at the tip of the promontory.

They advanced from desert garden (oasis) to desert oasis until finally they arrived at the red granite mountains of Sinai. Obviously, they were protesting and grumbling a significant part of the time. They were sick of eating nourishment (manna)! They were worn out on voyaging! Why, goodness why, had they given Moses a chance to talk them into this?

At Mount Sinai

Mount Sinai is a noteworthy milestone or "landmark" in the southern part of the Sinai Peninsula. Yet, the majority of all, it is a "milestone" or "landmark" in Hebrew history. Sinai is where Jehovah made an "agreement" or "contract" with the Hebrews. Through this agreement, Jehovah became their God and they became his people. From that day on, Jehovah and these Hebrews would belong to one another.

Exodus 19:3-8. What do these verses disclose to us Jehovah had accomplished for the Hebrews? What does he need to accomplish for them now? What must they accomplish for him? Two promises like these made up a "covenant."

"I Am Your God"

Jehovah was the Hebrews' God. That was the significant thing. He generally would be their God. Now they had a place with him (they belonged to him), and they generally would have a place with him and to no other god. Presently there must be no moon god, no sun god, no river god for these people only the "True and Living God, Jehovah."

Moses told the people what Jehovah had accomplished for them and what he demanded of them. They should be devoted to Jehovah and to his laws. At that point Moses addressed Jehovah for the Hebrews to promise that they would be devoted (faithful) to him. The Hebrew people would need to fall in line!

Exodua 20:1-17. When Jehovah became their God at Mr. Sinai, the Hebrews realized that they should be steadfast (faithful) to him and comply (obey) with his laws. What we read here was composed many, many years after the fact, obviously.

Dr. John Thomas Wylie

It is a part of this story, however, in light of the fact that the Hebrews consistently remembered that they started to obey Jehovah when he made his agreement (covenant)with them at Sinai. For what reason would you call verses 2a and 3 the "first and greatest commandment"?

We generally consider Moses and Jehovah's commandments together. Furthermore, that is correct, despite the fact that many laws of the Hebrews grew up long after the great event at Sinai had occurred. When the Bible stories came to be recorded, however, the Hebrew scholars connected all their most significant laws with Moses. This discloses to us that they generally thought of Moses as Jehovah's lawgiver for their country. It discloses to us that they realized Jehovah consistently had wanted them to pursue his way for them.

The Solemn Ceremony At Sinai

This covenant Jehovah made with the Hebrews required a grave strict service. A special raised altar was set up at the foot of the mountain. All people accumulated around it. At the point when animals had been slaughtered for a sacrifice,

Moses again advised the people what Jehovah wanted to accomplish for them and what they should accomplish for him. Once more, the people vowed to serve Jehovah and to obey him (Exodus 24:3-11).

Definitely this was the most magnificent minute in an incredible entirety. He was certain that Jehovah had helped him and his people along at all times. Every one of the people knew this, as well, and they had promised consistently to serve and obey Jehovah.

This made every one of the issues of the past blur away. Truth be told, this brilliant thing couldn't have occurred without every one of the troubles and issues they had. This was sufficient to cause Moses to overlook the occasions that the people had protested at him and at Jehovah. The entirety of that was past at this point.

Would the Hebrews truly satisfy their promise? Would they generally be steadfast (devoted, faithful) to Jehovah?

Rebels In The Wilderness

Would the Hebrews be devoted to Jehovah? The response to this was not long in coming. The minute Moses left the people to go up into the mountain where he felt near Jehovah, they chose to make a divine being (idol god) for themselves! In Egypt they generally had images to give them what their divine beings resembled. Is there any valid reason why they shouldn't have one at this point?

Moses' brother, Aaron, helped the Hebrews accomplish this horrendous thing. Utilizing every one of the people groups' gold ornaments, he made a symbol that resembled a youthful bull. Maybe the Hebrews had worshiped a bull-god in Egypt. Or then again maybe they imagined that Jehovah resembled one of the bull-divine beings (idol gods) that their neighbors venerated (Exodus 32:1-24).

Regardless of what they had thought or why they had made their object of worship, Moses realized that the people had broken Jehovah's covenant. They would need to be forgiven for that. We make certain of that, as well, but the following thing that happened appears to be awful to us. "The bull-admirers (bull worshipers) must be murdered!" (See Exodus 32:25-29).

How could such a horrendous thing be? To every one of the people of the ancient world, the appropriate response was straightforward. "If we didn't murder these crooks," they would let us know, "our divine beings would not pardon our clan. We are being faithful to our divine beings and to our clan when we dispose of these troublemakers." The Hebrews, obviously, accepted this, as well.

It would be quite a while before the Hebrews would discover that God needs to forgive and assist each person with trusting and obeying him.

The Sacred Ark

The Hebrews never would have an image to advise them that Jehovah was their God. In any case, they had something to remind them that he was with them when they assembled the "Ark of the Covenant." We don't know exactly what this Ark resembled; the portrayal of it in the Bible was composed long after the Ark itself had vanished.

Anything that it resembled, however, it was the Hebrews' most hallowed belonging. They believed that Jehovah himself sat or rode concealed upon it. The Ark was his sacred place (See Exodus 25:1-22; 37:1-10).

This appears to be abnormal to us, for we have

come to know that God is everywhere. Be that as it may, it didn't appear to be abnormal to the ancient Hebrews. Every one of the people of that day believed that their divine beings (idols) had a place with a specific land or people and lived in a specific place.

So their consecrated Ark reminded the Hebrews that Jehovah was their God; it reminded them that he generally was with them to support them. What's more, it reminded them that they should consistently be submissive (obedient) to him.

Any place the Hebrews went, the hallowed Ark of Jehovah was carried before them. Clerics (Priests) conveying the Ark on posts on their shoulders led the way. Afterward, when they would need to battle their way through disagreeable region, they would carry the Ark with them into fight. They would be certain then that Jehovah was with them to battle for them.

We don't know exactly when the Hebrews moved from their camping place close to Mt. Sinai. Our story reveals to us that the Hebrews who left Egypt currently went through forty years moving here and there in the wilderness. At the point when we read that none of the adults who left Egypt lived to enter Canaan, that would appear to be about right.

For what reason did it take such a long time? The essayists of our story discloses to us that the people were being rebuffed for defying (disobeying) Jehovah. They didn't merit anything better! The Hebrews were an inconvenient people!

Quite a while were spent at a desert garden called Kadesh-barnea, an eleven-day venture from Mount Sinai. Indeed, even in this alluring, admirably watered campground there consistently appeared to be inconvenience among the people. Moses more likely than not thought about whether they ever truly would comprehend what Jehovah expected of them (Numbers 20:1a).

When finally they left Kadesh, the Hebrews went poorly as we would anticipate. They went south to Ezion-geber once more, the place acclaimed for its copper mines. From that point the Hebrews more likely than did whatever it takes not to go straightforwardly north by way for a course called the King's roadway. The Edomite clans who lived there would not give them a chance to go through their region, however. (See 20:14-21).

So by and by the vagabonds wanted to utilize

a crisscross course. They without a doubt never expected to have such huge numbers of hindrances in their manner this late in their voyage! Would they ever get to Canaan?

At long last they requested that permission to follow the King's Highway the land that is known for the Amorites; yet again they were rejected authorization. These Amorites truly signified "no" when they said "No," for they sent a military to pound the Hebrews.

Be that as it may, this time the tables were turned! This time the Hebrews won! It was their first military triumph. Actually, they were triumphant to such an extent that they assumed control over the whole realm of the Amorites (21:21-25).

After the primary achievement, the Hebrews pushed on toward the north. Before long they won their way through a greater amount of this domain. Bit by bit they were coming nearer to Canaan!

Moses' Last Days

At this point Moses was an elderly man. He had seen numerous adjustments in his people during these long periods of wandering. There had been murmurers who consistently were wanting the great fish and cucumbers and melons they had delighted in Egypt. There had been troublemakers who didn't care for Moses.

A portion of the people consistently had been apprehensive and would have gone back to Egypt. Be that as it may, now, the vast majority of these had vanished. A more youthful, more courageous, harder age had taken their place.

When Moses realized that he didn't have any longer to live, he gathered together the elders of the people. They met at the foot of Mount Nebo, only east of the Promised Land. It was the ideal opportunity for Moses to find another leader for the people. He had brought them to the extent he could.

The greater part of all, Moses wanted to remind his people one final time of the covenant Jehovah had made with them. He wanted to reveal to them again how Jehovah had brought them out of Egypt. He wanted to ensure they would obey Jehovah's laws perpetually (Deu. 31).

Leaving his people down on the plain, Moses at that point moved to the pinnacle of Mount Nebo. From that point he could see over the

Jordan. From the highest point of the mountain Moses looked down on an amazing perspective on the Promised Land.

There it lay, spread at his feet, the land that once had been the home of Abraham, Isaac, and Jacob! There it was, the land to which he had been traveling with these Hebrew people as far back as their departure from Egypt! Jehovah had brought him and his people here, Moses was certain.

Deuteronomy 34:4-6. What does verse 4a reveal to us Jehovah consistently had wanted for the Hebrew people?

Moses was seeing this land with his very own eyes, however he could never go there himself. He had reached the end of his long adventure. Be that as it may, for his people, it was only the beginning. How might they toll with their new leader, Joshua, when they attempted to win this land for their home?

Chapter Four

Winning The Land

HOME! HOW GREAT THAT word more likely than not sounded to the destitute drifters. Only a river currently remained between the Hebrew people and their dream. At the point when they crossed the Jordan, they would be "home" for good. Presently it was up to their new leader, Joshua, to complete the task Moses had started.

Over The Jordan

"What is it truly like over yonder?" the Hebrews more likely than not pondered. Nobody truly knew, not by any means the covert agents (spies) who had been sent into the land to bring back reports. Obviously, the people currently living there would not let them simply come in.

Everybody realized that. They would need to battle for a home in Canaan similarly as they needed to battle en route. In any case, would they be sufficiently able to win the land?

How should Joshua and the Hebrews have felt as they looked over the Jordan into this obscure land?

Joshua 1:1-11. The storywriters were certain that Jehovah wanted to enable the Hebrews to win their way into Canaan. What did the Hebrews believe they should do with the goal that Jehovah would support them?

How did the people of Canaan feel about this swarm of outsiders outdoors there over the Jordan? They had caught wind of the Hebrews' fights and triumphs on their way toward Canaan, our story lets us know.

Now they stood by uneasily in their fortification towns, thinking about whether these people over the Jordan would attack their land. If that occurred, they would need to battle to keep their homes. In any case, consider the possibility that the God of these outsiders was more dominant than their very own baals, the divine forces (Idol gods) of Canaan.

What a terrifying idea! Maybe the Jordan River would shield these Hebrews from getting into Canaan. During this season the Jordan's banks ought to be overflowed. The Jordan would be difficult to cross.

Crossing The Jordan

When The Hebrews went to the banks of the Jordan, they stayed outdoors there for three days. At that point, without wetting their feet, they walked directly over the river into Canaan! What had occurred (Joshua 3:14-17)?

Maybe a seismic tremor or the downpours had caused an avalanche upstream. This would have dammed up the waters. A wonder such as this has been known to occur every now and then, but whatever caused the stream bed to be dry, the Hebrews were certain that Jehovah had helped them once more.

This was the minute for which everybody had paused. The Hebrews finally were in the land that they before long would call their own! That night they worshiped Jehovah in Canaan just because (4:19-24).

Capturing Jericho

It had been anything but difficult to get into Canaan, but the Hebrews' following stage couldn't be simple. Jericho, an ancient fortification city (a fortress), stood directly in their way. Now what?

How intense the Hebrews were to make Jericho their first military objective! They never had attempted to capture any city, and this one had high, well-protected walls, their story lets us know. Jericho would need to be taken.

One morning as the people of Jericho watched out over their city's walls, they saw Joshua's military out on the plain. In the event that from the outset they were startled, following a second look they more likely than not been diverted. There, driving the quiet, walking men, were the Hebrew priests, blowing trumpets!

"What new sort of weapon is this?" the people of Jericho more likely than not chuckled. "Do they plan to battle with those? Will their trumpets separate our hefty walls?"

How could Joshua and his men ever would capture Jericho?

Maybe it was another seismic tremor that made the city's walls disintegrate. Down through the ages, tremors have been serious in the Jordan Valley. Whatever we may think today, however, when the Hebrews saw the walls of Jericho self-destruct, they yelled, "Jehovah has done this for us!"

As they cleared up into the unprotected city,

they were certain that Jehovah had helped them win their first genuine hang on the place where there is Canaan. "Before long all the land walked into the slope nation. Could their expectations be correct? Might they be able to rapidly catch city after city until all the land would be theirs?

Defeat At "The Ruin"

A couple of miles west of Jericho, the Hebrews battled again to catch "simulated intelligence." yet this time they fizzled. What a blow that was to their expectations! What had occurred?

At the point when issue like this came to them, people of the old world accepted that their divine beings (gods) had gotten it going to rebuff them for some off-base they had done. That was exactly what Joshua believed at this point.

Jehovah had not battled with the Hebrews this time, he was certain, on the grounds that somebody had violated his laws and aggravated him. There was just a single activity. The swindler must be found and rebuffed (punished).

To discover who was to be faulted, Joshua had the Hebrews "make bets." Today we would call this "flipping a coin" or "drawing straws" to discover the "loser." That was the route people of the old world believed their divine beings (gods) disclosed to them who ought to be punished.

In our story, it worked out that one of the men had kept a portion of Jericho's fortune for himself. That was every one of the Hebrews had to know. At that point they accomplished a ghastly thing. They battered the man to the point of death and his significant other and children, as well. They were certain that Jehovah resented the man. They were similarly as sure that Jehovah must resent the man's family, as well (Joshua 7:6-26).

What an awful thing to believe! What's more, what a horrible activity! Could God truly have wanted them to do it? We know the response to that, obviously. It would require some investment to discover that God cares about every person.

It would require some investment to discover that God needs to excuse and assist every individual with trusting and obey him. Some time, however, they would come to know this, similarly as they previously had come to know that they should obey Jehovah.

On Into The Land

After the Hebrews had punished the traitor and his family, they were certain that Jehovah would help them once more. They were much increasingly certain about that when they captured the city where they had been crushed previously.

We know today that his city truly was Bethel, not Ai. Ai had been crushed hundreds of years before the Hebrews at any point came into Canaan, archeologists have found. In any case, Bethel, a town near the abandoned hill of Ai, was decimated at this very time.

The essayists of our story recalled the place but not the name of the town. It is no big surprise they called the spot "Ai," however; Ai signifies "the ruin." After their triumph, Bethel was left in ruins (8:1-29).

From here on it is difficult to tell precisely what occurred during nowadays. Did the Hebrews move through the entire land, winning fights and catching urban areas as they went? One story in the Bible appears to disclose to us this. In any case, another story appears to state that they had a long, hard time winning their way into Canaan.

Every one of these accounts were composed long after the occasions they tell about, obviously, so we can see what number of things would have been overlooked.

We are recounted numerous fights that were battled. After Bethel was caught, Joshua's warriors crushed the militaries of five rulers in southern Canaan. Archeologists have filtered through the cinders of the very flames that obliterated Libnah, Lachish, and Eglon at that point.

After this, some significant urban communities of northern Canaan were caught, as well. There, archeologists have dove into the cinders of the fire that set Hazor ablaze. The Hebrews finally had won their way into Canaan, both in the south and in the north. Jacob's relatives were in their own land once more.

Joshua more likely than not been a smart general to lead his people to such huge numbers of triumphs. With the exception of his administration, the Hebrews could scarcely have beat the Canaanites. His planning compensated for any quality his military needed.

He had sent government agents (spies) into Jericho before he assaulted there. He had utilized a smart trap to deceive the Canaanites at "Ai."

Dr. John Thomas Wylie

The Hebrews who battled with him were certain that Jehovah had helped their leader.

"That is the reason we won such a significant number of fights," they would have let us know. The essayists of our story, as well, were certain that Jehovah had helped Joshua and his officers win every one of the triumphs they tell about. "Jehovah constantly wanted us to live in our very own land," they would let us know. "This was the means by which he helped us when we returned into Canaan.

Sacrifices To Jehovah

The Hebrews were certain that Jehovah had helped them win their fights. They were similarly as certain about something different, as well. They were certain that Jehovah needed them to murder every one of the Canaanite people and to devastate every one of the homes of these urban areas that they caught. How could that be?

Could God truly have wanted the Hebrews to slaughter every one of the people and offspring of these urban communities they took? Could God truly have wanted them to set the entirety of Canaan's fine urban communities ablaze? This is exactly what they had done at Jericho and at Bethel and at Hazor and up and down the way. "This is the thing that Jehovah wanted us to do," they let us know!

The appropriate response might be difficult for us to see, but it was plain to the Hebrews. It was similarly as plain to the people they prevailed. Every one of the people of that day accepted that their divine beings (idol gods) "loved" them yet "despised" their foes, the Hebrews were certain that the Canaanites were adversaries of Jehovah.

They believed that Jehovah battled with them against the Canaanites and their divine beings (idol gods). So when they won a triumph, they believed that Jehovah truly had won it for himself and for them. "All that we catch has a place with Jehovah," they would have let us know.

That is the reason the Hebrews butchered their foes and consumed their urban communities. They thought of these people and urban communities as sacrifices to Jehovah. At the point when they accomplished this horrendous thing, they believed that they were being faithful to Jehovah.

Canaan was to be Jehovah's property (land). There could be no room in it for other people of

Dr. John Thomas Wylie

different divine beings (idol gods). There was only a single activity, they were certain, and that was to forfeit everybody and everything in it to Jehovah.

How Long Will It Be?

This appears to be awful and barbarous to us. For what reason do we have such an alternate thought of what God wants of us as we live in our reality with other people today?

The appropriate response truly is straightforward. It is the motivation behind why we are pondering God's way in the Old Testament. These Hebrew people who were so faithful to Jehovah were just starting to comprehend what God resembles and what he wants of us.

There was much-extremely, much-that God still would need to show them about his love for them and for everybody. At that point they would comprehend what he truly wanted them to accomplish for him.

What might God still need to do to support them-and us-come to know him as he truly may be? What's more, to what extent would it be?

There Was Peace, Too

The story of the Hebrews coming into Canaan was not every one of the one of fights and bloodshed and yielded urban communities. Each country appears to recollect more about the fights it has won than about its seasons of harmony!

Canaan was loaded with urban communities, and numerous or the vast majority of these were not taken in fight. Archaeologists have found that the Hebrews of Joshua's time settled in numerous Canaanite urban communities which they didn't obliterate. In numerous spots they just moved in to live calmly (peacefully) among the people who as of now were in the land!

Covenant At Shechem

Something occurred at Shechem late in Joshua's lifetime may reveal to us why the Hebrews could settle calmly in numerous parts of Canaan.

Joshua 24:1-28. This helps us to remember the contract (covenant) that had been made at Mount Sinai in Moses' day. Joshua told the tribes what Jehovah had done; at that point the tribes that were assembled at Shechem promised that they generally would serve and obey Jehovah.

It is peculiar to find that something like this occurred at Shechem. The Hebrews who came into Canaan with Joshua never had caught this city. Truth be told, they never had battled against any of the people who cherished in this parts of Canaan. But at this point every one of these people were promising to serve Jehovah. How could that be?

These people who lived in northern part of Canaan more likely than not been tragically deceased family members of the recently shown up Hebrews. They more likely than not been Habiru clans who never had been away from their country. Or then again maybe they were tribes who had returned to Canaan from Egypt when the Hyksos lost power there.

Or on the other hand maybe they were Habiru tribes who had come into Canaan after the first Hebrews had moved into Egypt. Anyway that might be, they had succeeded in Canaan. Here they had recounted and retold the narratives they recalled about Abraham and Isaac and Jacob-and Elohim.

Now, at this ceremony at Shechem, these

Habiru tribes of the North got together with their family members who had taken such a long time to get back home from Egypt. Now they, as well, vowed to serve Jehovah and to be faithful to him as it were.

The Hebrews couldn't have picked a superior place for this consecrated service. At the point when Abraham, their first ancestor, had come to Canaan quite a while in the past, he had revered at this very place! Shechem consistently would be a unique place to the Hebrews (Genesis 12:6-7).

Maybe this was the point at which all the Hebrew clans came to be designated "Israel." The story in the Bible uses that name for them now. In our story, however, we will continue calling the entirety of Jacob's relatives "Jews."

Living In The Land

Anyway they came to settle in their new homes, we now locate the Hebrew tribes dispersed all through Canaan, living in their Promised Land.

The tribes of Reuben and Gad lived on the high plain east of the Jordan. The tribes of Ephraim and Manasseh, Issachar and Zebulun, and Naphtali and Asher lived in the slopes of northern Canaan.

Ephraim was the biggest or most significant

tribe of the North. In the South were the tribes of Judah and Benjamin and Simeon, with the Levites living among them. Judah was the most significant tribe of the South.

The tribe of Dan, which from the outset lived close to the shoreline of the Great Sea, in the long run settled in the North around the city which they named for themselves. The Promised Land was never again a far away dream; now it was the Hebrews' land.

All things considered, not all of Canaan was settled by the Hebrews during Joshua's lifetime. There were numerous urban communities that the Hebrews just couldn't capture. One of these was Jerusalem. At that point, the Hebrews had not in any case attempted to capture the urban areas on the moving fields that slanted down to the sea from the mountains. They had no real way to battle against the chariots of the Canaanites.

So, they didn't approach the land close to the Mediterranean coast where the strong "People of the Sea," the Philistines, lived. It would be many years after Joshua died before the Hebrews would win the entirety of the Promised Land. However, they had done all around ok for now. So they settled down to living in the region that now was theirs.

When they had been only slaves in Egypt. Who could have speculated that in such a brief span this land could have come to be theirs! How had it occurred? "Jehovah did this for us," they were certain.

Trials In Canaan

For a long time after Joshua's death, there was no other strong leader of all the Hebrew tribes. What's more, this was exactly when they needed such a leader. The countries and tribes around the Hebrews wanted simply to drive them out of Canaan.

As time went on, these in people attempted ordinarily to recover their old homes or to remove urban communities that the Hebrew tribes had won from another person. That implied war. In any case, there was no strong leader to energize all the Hebrew tribes to confront risk together.

We read the account of these war-filled a very long time in the Book of Judges. It is one of the most energizing stories in all the Bible. There is an exceptional purpose behind this; it is comprised of a few short stories that various tribes told about their tightest breaks from danger.

Every one of these short stories tells how some strong head saved his tribe when it needed to battle for its very life. A portion of these accounts, as you could figure, talk about Yahweh; others discuss Elohim.

The leaders that these accounts tell about were designated "Judges." That is the way our story in the Bible got its name. These Judges were not attorneys who chose good and bad as our Judges do. They were armed force officers and strict leaders.

During nowadays when every one of the Hebrew tribes wanted to deal with itself, strong leaders like these judges were required. In the event that the tribes were cleared out individually, there never could be a Hebrew nation. It appeared that simply this was going to occur.

Jehovah's "Deliverers"

As a matter of first importance, a portion of the Hebrews were oppressed (enslaved) by their neighbors-until a leader named Othniel helped them win their freedom once more. At that point the Moabites southwest of Canaan became bosses of the Benjamin tribe until a left-gave leader named Ehud saved his people.

In northwestern Canaan the tribes of Zebulun and Naphtali were saved by a woman leader, Deborah. This time it took a woman "judge" to revitalize the Hebrew warriors to confront a multitude of Canaanite chariots.

Next, Midianite pillagers attacked focal Canaan-until it was saved by a leader named Gideon. From that point onward, Hebrews living east of the Jordan were subjugated by the Ammonites-until they were saved by another leader, Jephthah (see Judges 3:7-11; 12-30; 4:1-5:31; 6:1-8:25; 10:6-12:6).

So it went. At whatever point one enemy was beaten back, another immediately took its place. In any case, without fail, a strong Hebrew leader emerged to help save his threatened tribe.

Forgotten Promises

The essayists of our story let us know over and over that their ancestors had merited every one of these issues. Why?(Judges 3:7,8; 4:1,2; 6:1; 10:6,7). How could the Hebrews ever have overlooked Jehovah? Thinking back, we can perceive how it probably occurred. At the point when the Hebrews came into Canaan, they needed to get familiar with another lifestyle.

When they had lived in tents and moved here and there with their groups. Now, when they settled down to live in one place, they needed to figure out how to build houses and how to become farmers.

They took in every one of these things from the people who had lived in Canaan before them-their Canaanite neighbors. It is no big surprise that they figured out how to worship their divine beings (idol gods), as well. "These are the divine beings (idol gods) who carry downpour to this land and cause yields to grow here," every one of the Hebrews more likely than not been certain.

"We should make sacrifrices to them with the goal that they will support us, as well." Time after time, they overlooked the most significant thing they had learned-they neglected to be faithful to Jehovah. How could God ever use these people to show himself to all the world?

All things considered, God didn't give up on them. The essayists of our story were certain about this. They were certain that Jehovah remembered their ancestors despite the fact that they had overlooked (forgot) him. At last, they generally had been safeguarded.

Judges 3:9-11. The essayists were certain that Jehovah had saved the Hebrews since they had obeyed him once more.

What a superb thing it would have been for the Hebrews to see without further ado what this was teaching them regarding God. They had been leveled when they didn't have the right to be made a difference! It would be quite a while, be that as it may, before they would come to learn this and find out about God's forgiveness.

A Long Way To Go

At the point when we read the stories of these judges, we perceive how much the Hebrews still needed to find out about God. Gideon took gold adornments (ornaments) from the assemblages of killed Midianites-and made a holy image for his tribe to worship! His people still wanted to worship images! (Judges 8:24-27)

From that point onward, Jephthah yielded his daughter to Jehovah as an end-result of his triumph over the Ammonites! How could this be?

The Hebrews still believed that Jehovah wanted such sacrifices of them! It would be quite a while before the Hebrews could realize what God truly was like and what he wanted of them.

The Philistines

The Hebrews had a few enemies they never could survive. These were the Philistines. As per the Bible, the Philistines had been a nautical people who lived on islands close to Greece. ("Caphtor" in the Bible is Crete). They had attacked the entire eastern shore of the Great Sea.

With an armada of ships holding on, they had descended along the coast, vanquishing and pillaging. At the point when the Egyptians halted their development, the Philistines had settled in five urban areas along the coast-Ekron, Ashdod, Ashkelon, Gaza, and Gath. Now these people were ground-breaking to the point that the entire nation had come to be named "Palestine" for them. Palestine signifies "the Philistine area."

The Philistines were hard warriors. On numerous occasions they vanquished the Hebrews. At long last they threatened a Hebrew town, Aphek. In the event that they won Aphek, they effectively could proceed to take Shiloh, where the sacred Ark of the Covenant was kept.

"This can't go on!" the Hebrews started to cry. "There is only a single way to beat these people. We should get together, overlook our differences, and battle under a single leader!"

The settling-down long stretches of Canaan currently were ended. The age of the judges had kept going right around 200 years, but now it was attracting to a nearby. Gradually another thought was getting on-one Jehovah, one leader, one kingdom. How might everything come to fruition?

Chapter Five

A Kingdom Divided

A CLOUD OF DISTRESS and melancholy hung over the Hebrew people. The issue with the Philistines at Aphek had been the issue that crosses over into intolerability! How might they be able to ever overlook that place!

The Hebrews had been adequately beaten at Aphek not only once, but twice. The Philistines even had caught and diverted the sacred Ark of the Covenant. The Philistines had sent the Ark back not long after that; they were certain it had brought them awful disaster.

However, that didn't make the Hebrews feel greatly improved. It would not shield the Philistines from walking against them again at whatever point they wished. "For what reason is everything turning out badly for us?" the Hebrews needed to know.

Samuel, a priest whom every one of the Hebrews called a "prophet of Jehovah," immediately told the Hebrews what wasn't right. Such a large number of them were loving the land's baals, the divine forces (idol gods) of the Canaanites. Something must be done about that, and it must be done soon.

Samuel assembled the tribes at Mizpah. He was going to settle this baal business with Jehovah's people for the last time. There, at Mizpah, Samuel told the people again what Jehovah demanded of them. They should be totally faithful to him-and to him only. Indeed, what did the Hebrews need to say to that?

The Hebrew tribes addressed Samuel as their forefathers once had addressed Moses and Joshua and the judges. They vowed to surrender (give up) every single other god and to be faithful only to Jehovah once more.

At that, Samuel sent the Hebrews into battle; he was certain that Jehovah would battle with them now. The scholars of our story made certain of this as well, for their people vanquished the Philistines in their next huge fight.

No big surprise the Hebrews considered Samuel a "judge," as well. Be that as it may, what might befall them after Samuel was no more? Would they fall into difficulty again until another

Samuel came along to save them (see I Samuel 4:1b-11; 5:1-7:2; 7:3-14)?

Give Us A King

Huge numbers of the Hebrews were certain that they comprehended what should be finished. They should turn into a country like the various countries around them. A portion of the tribes previously had started to cry, "We should have a king, our own lord, to lead us." They were certain that a king would fend off inconvenience. In any case, would they say they were correct?

Different Hebrews were certain that it is inappropriate to have a king. "We should have no king but Jehovah," they said. We can't be too secure with the occasions that occurred straightaway. Maybe you as of now have speculated the explanation behind this.

We have two stories about the Hebrew ancestors. One of these accounts was told by the Hebrews who needed a king. These presumably were the people of the North. The other story was told by people who didn't need a king. They most likely were the Hebrew tribes of the South.

Both their accounts concede to a certain

something, however. If they would have a king, Samuel would be the man to choose him. Jehovah, and Samuel, as well, didn't care for the possibility of a king, one story lets us know (I Samuel 7:15-17). For what reason was that?

I Samuel 8:4-18. These verses are a part of a more extended story in 8:1-22 and 10:17-27. This is the story that may have been told by the southern tribes. What reasons do these Hebrews give for not needing a king?

Notwithstanding this, these people were certain Jehovah had advised Samuel to choose their first king for them, at any rate. Samuel assembled the tribes at Mizpah, they let us know. There he throw dice to find the man Jehovah would decide for them.

To us, obviously, this is by all accounts an abnormal method to choose a king. In any case, every one of the people of that day believed that "drawing straws" was a way their God addressed them.

"Yet, it wasn't that route by any stretch of the imagination," the people who wanted a king said again and again in their story. "Jehovah, and Samuel, as well, wanted us to have a king."

I Samuel 9:15-17. These verses are a part of

a more drawn out story in 9:1-10:16 that the northern tribes may have told. What reasons do these Hebrews give for wanting a king?

Maybe these people were correct. Maybe Samuel had furtively made Saul king when the imposing young man came to Ramah. Simply envision searching for jackasses and finding a kingdom!

Anyway it occurred, every one of the Hebrews made certain of this: they had their king now. That much was settled. Be that as it may, would it say it was going to harm them or help them? Who had been right about that?

The Hero King

The first response to this came rapidly. Some Canaanite neighbors in the east picked only this opportunity to threaten a Hebrew town with slavery or death. The Hebrews were in a difficult situation once more! Now they would check whether a king could save them.

Quickly, Saul called every one of the tribes to battle with him against these Ammonites. What a leader he ended up being! Furthermore, what a victory the Hebrews won! With the residue of fight still on them, the triumphant tribes rushed to Jehovah's haven at close by Gilgal. There they looked as Samuel freely made Saul their king. Now they would be prepared to take on the Philistines (I Samuel 11)!

Saul and his warriors didn't have long to trust that the Philistines will get vigorously. These "People of the Sea" before long heard that the Hebrews had a king who was driving them to victory in battle.

You can envision them saying among themselves, "How about we stop this king business of the Hebrews before it goes any further." But this time the Philistines were past the point of no return. A Surprise assault put them on the run (I Samuel 13:2-14:46)!

The Hebrews who had wanted a king probably been right all things considered! They were pleased with their king who ruled them from his capital in Gibeah.

The King Becomes A Problem

"A king may be good," other Hebrews may have conceded, "but Saul simply isn't the right ruler." they were certain. Saul had prevailed upon extraordinary triumphs his people's enemies. Be that as it may, he couldn't win the trust of all his very own people. He generally had realized that a few people didn't care for him-those southerners, particularly.

More terrible than that, he had made Samuel furious at him. When Saul himself had offered a sacrifice before battling the Philistines. "You ought to have waited for me to do that," Samuel had disclosed to him at that point.

Some other time he had not relinquished everybody in a captured city as Samuel had requested him to do. Once more, Samuel had let him know irately that he had resisted Jehovah-and flopped as king.

Saul was stressed. More awful yet, his stress made him suspicious and envious of everybody. "Where can that old prophet be?" Saul more likely than not pondered, "And what's going on with him?" If only Saul had known (I Samuel 13:2-15; 15:1-33; 15:34, 35).

Rival From The South

At the time, maybe nobody truly realized exactly what was occurring. A short time later, a few unique stories were told about what may have been going on there. These accounts were about a youngster from the South-and how he began on his approach to turn into the Hebrews' next king.

"At the point when he was only a shepherd kid," one story stated, "Samuel furtively blessed him to have Saul's place" (I Samuel 16:1-13). "Goodness, no!" another story said. "He went to Saul's court at Gibeah to play smoothing music for the grouchy king (I Samuel 16:14-23).

"He truly got his beginning as a youthful warrior in Saul's military," still another story stated, "and the issue among him and Saul began when the people said he was a superior soldier than Saul (I Samuel 18:5-7).

Anyway the issue between these two may have begun, Saul developed increasingly suspicious and envious of David. Almost certainly he regularly murmured, "I treated David like my very own child. I made him a secure in my military.

I gave him my little girl for a spouse. Presently, how can he compensate me? By attempting to take my kingdom from right in front of me!" It was obvious to Saul that he would be advised to dispose of David. That was the point at which they started a hazardous round of find the stowaway.

As Saul sought after him, David got away and covered up in one place after another everywhere throughout the kingdom. Regardless of each stunt that Saul attempted, however, David consistently escaped.

A few times he could have killed Saul, however each time he saved his life (I Samuel 19:18-26:25).

At long last Saul wanted to quit pursuing David. The Philistines had walked to the assault of the Hebrews in the North once more. How Saul wanted that Samuel were there to let him know, "Jehovah will fight with you." But Samuel had died some time in the past. Regardless of whether he could have addressed him, Saul realized what he would have said.

"You have failed," the old prophet had let him know previously. Saul realized that now, as well. He and his people of the North would need to battle alone; the tribes of the South would not support them. Saul had neglected to keep every one of the Hebrews together in one country.

Now, Saul felt isolated. He was certain that he would be crushed. The following day, his most noticeably terrible feelings of trepidation worked out. The fight, his position of authority, and his life-all were lost (I Samuel 31:1-13).

Another and more grounded leader was required somebody who might have the option to join the Hebrews and free them from the Philistines until the end of time.

A New King

Rather than cooperating now when they generally expected to, the tribes of the North and tribes of the South stressed more remote and more remote separated. These two gatherings always had been unable to get along well together.

The people of northern Canaan never could overlook that they were the old-clocks in the land. They had lived in their very own urban communities in their own territory "Israel" for ages. They looked down on the meandering warrior tribes that had originated from Egypt to settle in southern Canaan.

Yet, they paid special mind to them, as well. As of now that part of the land was classified "Judah" after the name of perhaps the most grounded tribe.

"Those upstart family members of our own down in Judah need to administer the entire nation," the people of the North were certain. There will undoubtedly be inconvenience now.

The southern tribes of Judah immediately made David their king. The northern tribes of Israel wouldn't pursue David. They needed a northerner for their leader, so they made one of Saul's children their king. After this, savage fights were battled between the armed forces of the two rulers, David and Ish- bosheth (II Samuel 2:4, 10).

At last Ish-bosheth and his general were slaughtered. At that point David became king of the considerable number of tribes similarly as Saul had been from the start.

Be that as it may, would the North follow David any superior to anything the South had followed Saul (II Samuel 5:1-3)?

A New Capital For The Hebrews

The new king wanted another capital city for his Hebrew nation. Hebron, his capital in Judah, was an excess of a part of the South for the northern tribes. What's more, obviously, Gibeah, Saul's old capital in Israel, was a lot of a part of the North.

The one place which David wanted, however,

would be difficult to get. Jebus-uru-salim was an ancient walled city on a mountain of rock. Regardless it was held by the Jebusites, a Canaanite people. No Hebrew leader, not in any case Joshua, at any point had the option to overcome it.

David's shrewdness won the city for him. David knew that the Jebusites' ablest warriors would monitor the city's strong walls. So he had his warriors creep up into the post through a water shaft.

This passage was protected distinctly by the weak and visually impaired (blind) elderly people men of the city. David's fighters caught the city effectively! The new king had his new capital city! Starting now and into the foreseeable future it would be called Jerusalem (II Samuel 5:6-10).

New Friends

When David had won Jerusalem, he hired Phoenician skilled workers from Tyre to build him a palace "a house of cedar." simultaneously, David made a settlement (treaty) with king Hiram, their ruler. From that time on, the Hebrews and the Phoenicians consistently would be companions (II Samuel 5:11).

The Last Of Old Enemies

David's other neighbors on the shore of the Great Sea were not amicable. These Philistines were concerned when they discovered that David was king of all the Hebrew tribes. They realized what a cunning general he was. At the point when Saul had driven him out of his own nation, he had lived and battled close by them for some time (I Samuel 27:1-4).

The Philistines immediately walked against the new Hebrew king. This time, David's military of northerners and southerners battling next to each other was a lot for them. Very soon the Philistines were driven back to their own boondocks, "from Geba to Gezer." From now on, the Hebrews would not need to stress over the Philistines any longer (II Samuel 5:17-25).

Jehovah's Place In Jerusalem

After David had built his fine, new royal residence (palace) in the country's capital, he and his men went walking off again toward the west. Their objective was a little town close to the old outskirt between the Hebrews and the place that is known for the Philistines. What would they be able to do? The Philistines had been driven back to the seacoast. That part of the kingdom found a sense of contentment now.

This strategic mission was the most significant one for David's entire life. The name of the town to which David was going provides us some insight into why he was going there. Baale-judah signifies "baals" or "lords of Judah." David was headed to the town where the hallowed (sacred) Ark of the Covenant was kept.

It had been in Baale-judah as far back as the Philistines had sent it back subsequent to taking it at Aphek some time before. Now David would carry the Ark to Jerusalem. A tent had been set up in an extraordinary spot in Jerusalem to protect it; a special stepped area (altar) had been built there for contributions to Jehovah.

At Baal-judah the Ark was stacked onto a ox drawn cart to carry it to Jerusalem. Be that as it may, in transit, a man tumbled to the ground-dead-when he reached out with to keep the Ark from being thrown off the lurching cart. This frightened David-and angered him. Now he was certain that the Ark could be hazardous. He left it at the very spot.

Afterward, David heard that the man on whose land the Ark had been left was getting wealthy. This sent David hustling out to the spot once more. Now he was certain that Jehovah would help any person who sheltered the sacred Ark.

This time David and every one of the Hebrews took the Ark back to Jerusalem with them (II Samuel 6:12-15). A long parade of moving, singing people carried it up into the walled city. Now, finally, it was in a position of honor once more.

Jehovah would want to be in the capital city of their land, the Hebrews were certain. There it generally would advise them that he was their God and that he had helped them to turn into a strong country in their very own land, Canaan. There it would advise them that they were his people and that they should serve him only.

Psalm 24:7-10. Maybe this tune was sung when the Ark of the Covenant was brought through the city gates of ancient Jerusalem. What verses disclose to you that the Hebrews were certain Jehovah had battled with them when they won Canaan for their own land? "Hosts" signifies "armies."

The Hebrews' Great King

With David as their king, the Hebrews before long vanquished the entirety of Canaan. That was what Joshua had started to accomplish in excess of 200 years prior (II Samuel 8:1-14). They were proud for their strong country.

They told this again and again in the tunes of thanksgiving they sang to Jehovah. Regardless we sing a portion of their melodies today, for they are among the psalms in our Bible.

"David our king showed us a large number of these melodies," the story authors let us know. They generally would remember that their extraordinary king was a poet and a musician.

The Hebrews consistently would be pleased with David, but they generally would remember his issues, moreover. He was bold and faithful, yet he likewise had been pitiless and deceptive. He butchered hostage Moabites. He had plotted the dying of a faithful companion with the goal that he could wed the man's beautiful wife.

He let seven children of his old enemy Saul be yielded when a starvation went to the land. A large portion of every one of, the Hebrews consistently would remember that David had repented Jehovah's forgiveness for his wrongdoings (sins).

Psalm 51:1-4. At the point when the prophet Nathan disclosed to David how he had trespassed (sinned) against Jehovah by murdering a man to get his significant other, David repented.

The Hebrews storywriters believed that these words enlightened how David felt concerning his transgressions (sins).

Take a look at verses 10-12. We sing these words in worship today.

Regardless of his flaws, it would be a long, long time before the Hebrews ever would have another leader like David.

David's Quarreling Sons

In any case, what might happen when David was no more? There consistently was desire and quarreling among his numerous spouses and every one of their children. His preferred child, Absalom, caused him the best pity of his life.

This child plotted cautiously to take the kingdom from his father. All of a sudden he struck, executing his very own several brothers. At that point David wanted to escape Absalom, his own child, similarly as he once had avoided Saul! However, David was grief stricken when this risky most loved child was killed (II Samuel 13:11-18:33)!

Who ought to be king after David? Could any of his quarreling children rule just as well as he had ruled?

Solomon-And All His Glory

At last, David's son Solomon became the Hebrews next king.

A story in the Bible tells how Solomon imagined that he approached Jehovah for shrewdness to be a good leader of his people. Every one of the people in Israel were proud for their shrewd, new king (I Kings 3:3-15).

Truth be told, they believed that he was more shrewd than every one of the men of his day. During that time they told and retold many astute adages they were certain no one but he could have thought of (I Kings 4:29-34).

Life was prosperous and tranquil during a large portion of the forty years that Solomon ruled. The country's adversaries of quite a while in the past still were powerless. Solomon had an incredible armed force, however it never needed to take on a genuine conflict.

Solomon and the country turned out to be exceptionally affluent during these quiet years. Presently a considerable lot of the Hebrew people were specialists and merchants. They had figured out how to accomplish more than cultivate and care for their flocks. The country turned out to be increasingly more rich through exchanging with different countries of their world.

This riches implied that Solomon could gather more duties from his people. To do that, the king isolated the nation into twelve locale. At that point he designated an official for each area to gather taxes. Each official additionally drafted men from his region who at that point needed to leave their homes to work for the rich king.

Things were greater, more excellent, and showier during Solomon's rule than they at any point had been previously. Indeed, even Jesus, a thousand years after the fact, spoke about "Solomon in all of his glory." Solomon arranged numerous enormous tasks that required a lot of cash and much hard work.

The city of Jerusalem was made greater. Solomon needed it to be the best, most extravagant city in the world! His own home took thirteen years to build; it was an illustrious royal residence that stunned all the outside rulers who came to visit in Jerusalem. Life in Solomon's court was more stupendous than anything the Hebrews at any point had seen under the watchful eye of at any ruler's court.

The House Of Jehovah

Solomon's most significant venture was to assemble a sanctuary (temple) for Jehovah. The prophet Nathan had said that David ought not build it. Engineers, metal specialists, and skilled workers were brought from Phoenicia to Jerusalem once more.

These Phoenicians were the most gifted manufacturers (builders) and skilled workers of that day. For a long time they took a shot at Solomon's "House of Jehovah." The best materials that could be gotten were used for it. It was made of enormous squares of exorbitant white limestone slashed by King Hiram's artisans.

Bars cut from the world-acclaimed cedars of Lebanon were used for its rooftop. Within walls were framed with cedar. The structure was adorned with valuable metals that David had taken from vanquished countries.

Solomon's people viewed the laborers construct this fine sanctuary (temple), stone by stone. "There never has been such an excellent sanctuary (temple)!" they marveled.

"Excessively costly!" murmured the exhausted farmers and merchants. What's more, the traders who made a trip to different terrains stated, "We've seen greater temples for other divine beings (idol gods), and they never cost as much as this!"

Be that as it may, in one unique way this sanctuary (temple) was not quite the same as whatever other sanctuary (temple) that at any point had been constructed. There was no picture of Jehovah anyplace in it-not even in the Holy of Holies. Just the hallowed Ark of the Covenant was kept in this special room.

Here it remained in obscurity, under the wings of two cherubim cut from olive wood and overlaid with gold. Nobody at any point went into this unlighted room with the exception of the High Priest.

Jehovah couldn't be seen! The Hebrews never would make a image of him. How bizarre this probably appeared to the Hebrews' neighbors-a temple without a image of a divine being in it!

Jews from everywhere throughout the land jammed into Jerusalem on the day when Solomon dedicated this sanctuary (temple). This was an exceptional, unforgettable day in the Hebrew country's history (I Kings 8:22-66).

Wise Or Foolish?

In spite of all the splendor and glory of Solomon's kingdom, things truly were not going great for his people. The Hebrews were surrendering increasingly more of their old ways, and they didn't care for it.

"The expense gatherers (tax collectors) remove a greater part of our yields at each reap," the farmers griped.

"For what reason are we compelled to deal with Solomon's structures and urban communities just as we were vanquished slaves?" other men needed to know.

An ever increasing number of the people started to ask, "What can the king consider?" Foreign rulers who came to visit Solomon's magnificent court considered him an insightful ruler; however his own people started to imagine that he was absurd and avaricious. Solomon's love for influence and riches were making life hard for his people.

In any case, that was not such wasn't right! As the years passed, Solomon took numerous foreign wives.

This was a manner by which he made arrangements with different countries. Be that as it may, as this occurred, he built sanctums (the shrines) in Jerusalem for the unusual divine beings (idol gods). He even started to worship at the altars of a portion of these divine beings (idols).

I Kings 11:1-8. Now Jehovah was not by any means the only god being worshiped in Jerusalem, the capital city of the Hebrews. What might this lead to?

I Kings 11:9-13. These verses give a trace of what might befall this country that had vowed to be faithful to Jehovah only.

Solomon's rule, for all its glory, was ending with disappointment, failure. What lay ahead for Jehovah's people? How could God use them to help the whole world come to know him if their king led them to worship other gods?

Chapter Six

A Kingdom United

REGARDLESS OF WHAT ANY other person thought, Solomon was certain that nothing wasn't right with his kingdom. Truth be told, it couldn't have satisfied him more.

His armada of boats still carried the wealth of the world to his seaports. A renegade in a tough situation down south, yet the rich mines and smelters there still gave riches to Solomon's treasury.

Another radical in the north had won back Syria's freedom, however Solomon's traders still made a trip to the grounds past to bring back more riches for the maturing king. His storage facility urban areas were loaded up with merchandise. Quick chariots could speed his military to wherever in the kingdom. Solomon's military never needed to battle a war, however.

Simply having such a strong armed force around was sufficient to maintain everybody in control. Solomon's people were apprehensive not to cover their regulatory obligations or to serve in the king's work posses.

In his sparkling castle in Jerusalem, Solomon had no stresses. The incomparable Temple for Jehovah was nearby. Solomon was certain that he had the cooperative attitude of different countries and their divine beings (idol gods), as well. His collection of mistresses of a thousand women was loaded up with foreign spouses; Jerusalem was specked with holy places to their foreign divine beings (idol gods).

Some time in the past the older folks of the tribes had gone to old Samuel to request a king. If no one but they could see the country and its capital city now! They would not have the option to believe what they saw. At that point they had been a herd of poor, terrified shepherds and farmers under the thumb of the Philistines.

Now they were the wealthiest country of all their general surroundings. Without a doubt Solomon had helped Jehovah's people progress significantly. Be that as it may, to where?

Grumbling From The North

A young man in the north of Israel could have disclosed to Solomon where the country was going. The old king would not have been eager to tune in. Jeroboam, this northerner, was one of Solomon's own young officials.

He was accountable for drafting men to work in the ruler's work groups. Be that as it may, Jeroboam, similar to every one of the people of the old northern tribes, was actually an agitator on the most fundamental level. He resented seeing Israel's riches and labor being depleted away to add to the glory of Solomon's capital city in Judah.

"We are the old-timers in this land," every one of the northerners thought. "Those newcomers in Judah who assumed control over our nation would be advised to watch out!" If the ruler at any point thought about what these people up north were thinking, despite everything he didn't stress, until...

One day Solomon heard news that bothered him. A prophet was influencing that youthful Jeroboam would become ruler of the northern tribes old Israel. That sort of talk must be settled quick. Quick chariots went speeding northward. Solomon's soldiers had orders to slaughter this man who may become king (I Kings 11:26-40).

Jeroboam moved still quicker, however. He ran away to Egypt. At that, Solomon disregarded him once more.

At the point when the old king died, Rehoboam, one of his numerous children, was chosen to follow him. In the event that solitary he had comprehended what lay ahead for his kingdom!

Trouble From The Start

Directly from the beginning Rehoboam more likely than not speculated that issue was en route. The elders had chosen that Rehoboam ought to be declared king in Shechem as opposed to in Jerusalem. That made him stress. Shechem was far toward the north, in the mountains of old Israel. Why Shechem?

Rehoboam's doubts deteriorated when he landed at this ancient city of the northern tribes. Jeroboam was there! What was Jeroboam doing at Shechem? Issue must mix. It was. The elders of Israel strongly confronted Rehoboam. "In what manner will you rule our country?" they inquired. To top it all off, Jeroobam was one of the examiners!

Would the new ruler (king) bring down the charges (taxes)? Would he quit drafting Israel's people to work for him? Would he treat the northern tribes of Israel just as he treated the tribes of Judah in the south?

For three days Rehoboam put off replying. He required the counsel of his nearby wise men.

The savvy elderly men of his court guided him to make life simpler for these people. In any case, Rehoboam's young friends instructed him to give them who was boss directly from the beginning. What would it be a good idea for him to do? What might he do? On the third day, Rehohoam furnished them his response.

I Kings 12:1-14, Whose "side" OK have been on? Why?

An Answer That Split A Kingdom

Rehoboam's words seemed like a long jail sentence toward the northern tribes. He had demanded much a greater amount of them than Solomon had!

That was such the ten tribes of the north need to hear! They would not represent it. "For what reason should we be administered by the house of David?" they cried. "We are not Judeans! To your tents, men of Israel (I Kings 12:16-29)!"

All the awful sentiments of the northerners toward the southerners finally had reached a critical stage. Now the Hebrew tribes were set to head out in their own direction once more. The ten tribes of old Israel made Jeroboam their king. Rehoboam was left with just the southern tribes of Judah and Benjamin.

Back in Jerusalem, Rehoboam acted rapidly for once. He would show Jeroboam and those northerners what a genuine king did to rebels. He and his warriors prepared to walk against Israel. Before they got going, they were halted. A prophet told the people of Judah that they were not to battle against their "brothers" in Israel (I Kings 12:24)!

Bad News Travels Fast

Word that Solomon's affluent country had self-destructed before long spread around the Fertile Crescent. It was simply tricky Shishak, Pharaoh of Egypt, had been standing by to hear. Promptly, he sent Egypt's military dashing toward Canaan.

Rehoboam immediately built a chain of invigorated towns around little Judah, but he couldn't stop Shishak's more grounded armed force. Judah was saved, but just when Rehoboam stripped the Temple of its fortunes and offered them to the Egyptian Pharaoh (I Kings 14:25-28).

What a narrow escape that had been! What's more, what a terrible blow it was to Jehovah's people! Did it imply that Jehovah was not as powerful as the Egyptian god, Amon?

Or on the other hand did it imply that Jehovah had lost control with his people in light of the fact that such a large number of were worshiping other divine beings (idol gods)? The storywriters were certain this was the explanation behind Judah's issue.

Now Judah would need to continue paying tribute to Egypt-or something bad might happen. Could God any more extended use this frail little country to help the world come to know him? Or then again would God currently use the ten tribes of Jeroboam new Israel to reveal himself to his world?

The story-path of the Hebrew people isolated

now. Now there would be two streets to pursue rather than one. Would these two streets ever meet again? Or then again would they take Judah and Israel more remote and more remote separated? What's more, which country would God use? or then again would he use both?

Jeroboam's Kingdom

While Rehoboam's Judah was experiencing its difficulty with Egypt, Jeroboam approached making his new country more grounded. Israel was so enormous and strong that it didn't need to stress over the Egyptians.

In any case, Jeroboam before long found that despite everything he needed to stress over little Judah. How could that be? His people detested the new king who ruled there.

Jehovah's Temple at Jerusalem was the issue. In the event that no one but Jeroboam could cause his people to overlook that place. In any case, even Shechem, his new capital, reminded the Israelites that some time in the past they had vowed to serve Jehovah and only Jehovah.

This very city was the place their forefathers originally had made that promise. What could

Jeroboam do about much of this? He couldn't help thinking that his people were acting more like Judeans than Israelites!

Jeroboam immediately moved his base camp to Penuel. However, that was insufficient. The people still were attracted to the Temple at Jerusalem. That was the place Jehovah abided unseen in the Holy of Holies, upon the consecrated Ark of the Covenant (I Kings 12:25-27).

What did Israel have that could be as critical to them as Jehovah's Ark in the Temple at Jerusalem? Nothing!

At last a thought came to Jeroboam. Israel must have its own places of worship. At that point the people would remain at home to worship. Jeroboam picked two places for his hallowed places Dan and Bethel.

Dan was on Israel's northern wilderness at the foot of Mt. Hermon. As far back as the times of the judges there had been an unrefined worship place there. Now Jeroboam would make it a splendid place. The Northern most tribes could go there with their sacrifices.

Bethel was uniquely around ten miles north of Jerusalem. It had been a sacred place of the Canaanites for as far back as men could remember.

In the times of the judges and of Samuel, it had been a most loved meeting place of the tribes.

Maybe Jeroboam picked it, since it was where the Israelites' stories about Jacob had been told again and again.

Behold Your Gods

Jeroboam's plans appeared to be good. For what reason couldn't Jehovah be worshiped similarly also at Bethel and at Dan as at Jerusalem? This would have been a brilliant new thing for the Hebrews to find out about God.

Something was the issue with what occurred. Jeroboam put in every one of these altars of a gold statue of a bull-calf. "Here are the divine beings (idol gods)," he told the people, "Who brought you out of the place that is known as Egypt" (I Kings 12:28-33). I'm not catching this' meaning?

Jeroboam may have thought of Jehovah as standing concealed upon the backs of the gold images. The people of Canaan frequently had images of a baal standing on the back of a youthful bull. In any case, this lone opened the entryway to let in other wrong thoughts regarding

Jehovah and the manner by which he ought to be worshiped.

Gradually the people started to mix up Jehovah with the baals. As the years went on, the people started to float more distant and more remote away from Jehovah and his laws.

Could God ever utilize these people to help the world to know him?

From Bad To Worse

One king after another ruled in Israel-ten of them in a hundred years. These new kings brought other new thoughts and customs into Israel. Their foreign spouses additionally acquired new thoughts, and these were not in every case smart thoughts either!

This was particularly obvious when ruler Ahab brought his Phoenician wife, Jezebel, to Israel. Genuine inconvenience started when she originated from Sidon to the fine new capital that Ahab's father had built in Samaria.

Queen Jezebel carried her own religion with her. More awful than that, she anticipated that the people of Israel should worship her god, Baal-Melkart. Ahab had a sanctuary for this Baal built in Samaria. Most likely it was particularly similar to Jehovah's Temple in Jerusalem, for it was worked by Phoenician skilled workers, as well.

I Kings 16:29-34. These verses reveal to us how the Hebrews obtained the religions of their neighbors. How did our essayist feel about a Hebrew king wedding a "foreigner"? For what reason would he say he was certain this was so awful? What other Hebrew king had done this?

Verse 34 tells how a Hebrew relinquished two of his sons to devote the establishment and doors of a reconstructed Jericho. This was an old agnostic custom. Maybe this kind of thing made other Hebrews remember to the account of Abraham and Isaac in Genesis 22:1-14.

The people of Israel ran to the sanctuary of this foreign baal. In the event that this kind of thing kept on, God most likely couldn't use Israel to reveal himself to his world. Would this terrible thing be halted before it was past the point of no return?

The Man Who Dared Say "Stop!"

One day an irate Israelite named Elijah remained before Ahab to support Jehovah. That was risky! Could this irate man convince Israel's people to worship Jehovah once more? Little possibility! Since he had set out to criticize the king, he needed to escape and cover up to save his life (I Kings 17:1-5).

Elijah escaped none too early. At the point when dry spell and starvation struck the land, Jezebel was certain that Elijah and his Jehovah had carried this issue to Israel. She at that point had her servants execute every one of the "prophets" of Jehovah that they could find. Only Elijah and a hundred other steadfast prophets got away.

What a miserable situation this was! Jehovah required prophets to support him transparently where all the country would hear. Be that as it may, how could the people hear what Jehovah needed to state to them when every one of the prophets needed to remain sequestered from everything?

At the point when things appeared to be generally miserable, Elijah left covering up to face Ahab once more. This time he was angrier than any time in recent memory. "YOU are crushing Israel," he cried to the king. "You resist Jehovah's laws and follow Baal." Elijah censured the king for the dry spell that was demolishing the land.

Nobody could converse with the king like that and pull off it! Now what (I Kings 18:1; 17-18)?

The Contest On Mount Carmel

Now, our authors tell of one of the accounts that the Hebrews wanted to tell again and again. Elijah not just set out to confront the king; he requested to remain solitary against every one of the prophets of Jezebel's remote Baal!

They all would go to the old "high place" on Mount Carmel. There either Jehovah or Baal would send downpour (rain) in answer to their prophets' prayers. That would show who was Israel's god (I Kings 18:19)!

The prophets of Baal couldn't make their king have mercy on them. At that point Elijah approached Jehovah to show his power. What occurred next made everybody on Mount Carmel sure that Jehovah was far stronger than Baal.

Elijah's water-drenched sacrifice burst into fire. In an explosion of vengeance and reliability to Jehovah, the Israelites seized and executed the entirety of Baal's prophets. Before long the billows of a powerful tempest started to pour down downpour (I Kings 18:20-45).

Elijah's triumph didn't keep going long. At the point when Jezebel heard what had befallen the prophets of her baal, she irately pledged to dispose of this Elijah for the last time. Elijah needed to escape once more.

He didn't stop in his trip until he came to Mt. Sinai, or Horeb, as the Israelites called it. There, where Moses once had stayed, Elijah came to realize that he should return to Israel and serve Jehovah (I Kings 19:1-19a).

A Reformed Ahab

Back in Israel, it nearly appeared that Ahab had changed and become faithful to Jehovah. Twice, once in mountain nation and again on the plain around Aphek, he was certain that Jehovah helped his military thrashing attacking Syrians.

The subsequent thrashing was a genuine hit to the Syrians; they had been certain that Israel's Jehovah was a "lord of the slopes." They had not believed that he could help his people take on and win a conflict on the fields of Palestine!

Jezebel before long ruined everything. It started when a loyal Israelite would not offer his fine vineyard to Ahab. Land never was sold in

Israel. It generally gave from father to son. "Such stupidity," shouted Jezebel.

In her local Phoenicia, land could be sold or purchased whenever. "Try not to worry yourself," she told Ahab. "Your smart Phoenician wife will figure out how to get around that senseless Hebrew law." And she did. She plotted the death of the steadfast Israelite. At that point Ahab just took the vineyard for himself.

That was a lot for Elijah. The king and queen had broken one of Israel's most consecrated laws. Elijah's next message to the ruler was, "Both of you will have pay for this wrongdoing with your lives" (I Kings 21:1-24).

Another Missing Chapter

Did the people of Israel know what Elijah had told their king? If they did, they would have been certain that this next section in Ahab's life would be the last. Something difficult for them to accept was occurring.

The most odd thing about it to us, however, is the manner by which we find out about it. We don't discover it in the Bible story, however in the engraving on a landmark of a faraway ruler. What was happening, in any case?

Ahab was surging with his military to support the Syrians! Odd! As far back as Solomon's time, Syria had been attacking Israel and taking ceaselessly its urban communities. The residue from their last fights had barely settled. in any case, now Ahab was hustling to support Syria! Why?

Ahab still hated the Syrians, but he was increasingly terrified of a more grounded adversary from Abraham's old country.

This country, amazing Assyria, needed to become master of all Syria and Canaan-with the goal that it could get at Egypt. Except if Israel and Syria and the various little countries in its way stood together now, they all were damned.

A horrendous fight pursued at Qarqar, on the banks of the Orontes River. The protectors more likely than not set up a decent battle, for Assyria's military went directly back home once more. Be that as it may, for to what extent?

Together Again?

After this, Israel and Syria were up to their old deceives once more. This time Ahab began the fight; he attempted to win back urban areas that Syria had taken quite a while in the past. In the fight that pursued, Ahab lost his life.

Yet, in that equivalent fight, Israel was helped by another companion Judah! Were Jehovah's people meeting up once more? Were the two separate streets of Judah and Israel meeting once more?

The appropriate response isn't what we wish it may have been. Since Israel was so strong, Judah more likely than not went to support Ahab. We do know, that the scholars of our story didn't need the streets to meet once more. They were certain that Israel would make Judah unfaithful to Jehovah, as well (I Kings 22:1-36).

I Kings 16:29-33. The Hebrew storywriters had put these words at the absolute starting point of their story about Ahab. This story was composed after Israel had vanished as a country. The journalists were certain this had happened on the grounds that Israel's kings and people were not faithful to Jehovah. Who were these backstabbing leaders? What had they done?

Close To The End

Regardless of whether it was generally advantageous or not, the two streets didn't meet. A man named Jehu put a conclusion to any possibility of that. To make himself leader of Israel, he slaughtered Ahab's son, the king. The he slaughtered the remainder of Ahab's family and devotees in Israel, Jezebel above all else!

At that point he additionally executed Judah's above all else and numerous family members (II Kings 8:25-10:17). Now the two countries never would be companions. The streets had separated for eternity.

For a period it appeared that Jehu would have been faithful to Jehovah. By a smart stunt and a dreadful slaughter he decimated Baal's sanctuary (temple) and the entirety of Baal's priests and worshipers. In any case, this didn't make Jehu and the Israelites genuinely faithful to Jehovah (II Kings 10:18-31). They only needed to dispose of everything that helped them to remember Ahab and Jezebel, his foreign queen.

Jehu disposed of different tokens of Ahab's rule, as well. He broke every one of the settlements that Ahab had made with different countries. In any case, at that point, with no other countries to support them, the Israelites couldn't shield themselves any more. the Syrians looted their territory. At that point a greater and more grounded Assyria came to request tribute from failing Israel.

Was the Hebrew country in the North reaching the end of its street? What might the future hold for this country of Jehovah's people? Before long they would hear another sort of prophet revealing to them that the end was close. Who might then carry on for Jehovah?

Chapter Seven

Nations That Would Not Listen

AHAB AND JEHU HAD carried a wide range of issue to Israel. The people of the North more likely than not imagined that there would be no closure to it. At that point, shockingly, there came a time when things appeared to go well.

Another Jeroboam became king. Israel's old region was won back. Truth be told, the country currently arrived at its most noteworthy size. Jeroboam II added to Omri's work. Samaria, the capital, now was the best strengthened city in all Palestine. If only things could go on like this forever!

There were a few people among the Hebrews, who were certain that Israel didn't merit such favorable luck. Actually, these people were stating that Israel was damned. What a bizarre perspective that was! Be that as it may, these new prophets were odd (strange) people. The Hebrews never could think about what they would state straightaway.

Who were these new prophets? Also, what were they grumbling about in such prosperous times?

The Herdsman Of Tekoa

In the slope nation of Judah, a shepherd hung out sitting in the fields near Tekoa. Nobody could have speculated that he would be one of the new prophets. He never could have speculated that he additionally would be first to have his words recorded so that later ages would realize what he had said.

It was distinctly around twelve miles to Jerusalem from where Amos sat watching his runs. Amos was a country man, but he thoroughly understood the ways of city people. He needed to go to the urban communities frequently, to sell sycamore figs in their business sectors.

These figs were a poor, dull (tasteless) fruit, be that as it may, alongside his sheep, they helped Amos bring home the bacon. Once in a while he took his figs over Judah's fringe to Bethel, a bustling city in Israel. Bethel was the place the first King Jeroboam some time in the past had set up a golden calf image in its ancient sanctum (shrine).

Amos consistently felt similar to a poor relative when he went from his local Judah into one of Israel's fine urban communities. Israel was such a rich land. However, alongside this riches, Israel was loaded with destitution and hopelessness and despondency. How could this be? Amos pondered. At that point he started to see the appropriate response.

Israel resembled a few bins of fruit he had seen. Amos chose. The fruit over the bin was wonderful, yet underneath it was terrible, bad - right through. All through the land, the rich were bamboozling and abusing poor people. It wasn't right (Amos 8:1).

Somebody should state something or take care of such bad behavior. Amos more likely than not suspected. Maybe he himself should. Be that as it may, would anybody hear him out? He was just a poor, uneducated shepherd from the slopes of Judah. The sharp looking people of Bethel would snicker at him, in his course, unpleasant garments (rough clothes).

He Had To Be Heard

One day in Bethel, Amos couldn't be quiet any more. The city's tight boulevards were pressed with out-a-town people who had come to celebrate a feast. Like a man walking to battle, Amos pushed his way through the crowds.

He wanted to tell the people in Israel what he realized Jehovah needed them to hear. At the first clear space he discovered, Amos put down his pack. At that point he stood upright and started to talk.

"Listen, you people of Israel," Amos called out. A couple of people halted, at that point more. Before long a group was around him, listening to his irate words spill out. "What is this man saying?" a newbie inquired. "You ought to hear him," a fashionable man replied. "He's been discussing the murderous countries around our Israel. It's time that some upright Israelite stood up and came clean about them."

"Be that as it may, that person is a Judean," the late-comer said. The Well-dressed man looked again at Amos' harsh shroud. "So he is," he replied. "Yet, he's been stating exactly what I've thought for quite a while. He says Jehovah will make every one of these countries around us pay for their wrongdoings. They're a slanted parcel (a crooked lot)," he included indignantly (Amos 1:3-2:3).

The newcomer gestured in understanding. Everybody thought about the horrendous things Israel's neighbor countries had done. The two men went to listen to Amos once more.

Jehovah will punish Judah for getting some distance from his law," Amos roared (Amos 2:4,5).

The men's faces lit up with astonished, satisfied grins. This person was in any event, talking about his own people! It satisfied these Israelites to hear Amos say that Jehovah should punish Judah!

Amos' next words turned their grins to glares. They started to mumble brutal words through their facial hair (beards). Others in the group, as well, started to yell indignantly. What wasn't right? These people had been concurring with Amos; presently they plainly resented him.

Look Out Israel!

"Jehovah will punish you, Israel," Amos had stated, "on the grounds that you are a country of cheaters. You cheat poor people and the powerless and make captives of them. That is bamboozling Jehovah!"

The people in the group got some distance from Amos. He had aggravated them. This man from Judah was a trick and a troublemaker, they thought. In the event that occasions had been bad they may have listened to him, however not currently. Israel was strong and prosperous; didn't that mean Jehovah was satisfied with them?

Updates on what Amos had said before long got to king Jeroboam at Samaria. Envision a hill-country Judean coming into his well off Israel to state that the entire land was slanted (crooked)! To say the least, the king was furious. He wanted no untouchable raising hell in his tranquil land.

All things considered, the king may have ignored the entire thing, however then a priest from Bethel came rushing to him with all the more terrible news about the prophet from Judah. "Now he's colloquialism that Israel is set out toward ruin-banish," the priest reported.

"Exile, the king echoed. That could mean only a single thing. This untouchable implied that Assyria was going to attack Israel. Assyria had gotten incredibly, powerful in Abraham's old homeland (7:10,11).

"Pack up that nosy shepherd and send him back to Judah where he belongs," the king cried.

"What's more, let him know never to return!" The king trusted his people would before long overlook Amos' alarming words. Talk like that could disturb the entire kingdom (Amos 7:12-15)!

Amos' message was not going to be overlooked. Someone who had heard him speak knew that he was representing Jehovah. The unknown scribe recorded what Amos said. That is the reason we have his message even today.

New Truths About God

When we read Amos' message, we find something magnificent, something wonderful.

Amos had come to know a significant truth about God that the Hebrews had expected to learn. Amos realized that Jehovah wanted people to be right and honest and reasonable in all that they did on the grounds that Jehovah himself was that way.

Amos 5:21-24. The people of Israel believed that Jehovah wanted only their contributions and sacrifices. Amos knew that Jehovah wanted something different of them. Which verse says that Jehovah wanted the Hebrews to be right and honest and reasonable for with other?

We additionally find that finally many Hebrews had taken in another fact about God that they had expected to learn for such a long time. A few Hebrews like Amos come to know that Jehovah was the ONLY God of all the earth.

When they had believed that Jehovah was only their God; Now they realized that he was everyone's God. Amos had said that Jehovah was the God who might punish all the homicidal (bloodthirsty) countries around Israel. He even said Jehovah was God of the Egyptians, the Philistines, and the Syrians (Amos 1:2-2:3; 9:7)!

It would be a long, long time before every one of the Hebrews came to know this. Be that as it may, now, at any rate, a few Hebrews like Amos knew it. God could use these people to help other people come to know him and trust in him.

Maybe only a couple of sincere Hebrews saw every one of these things that Amos said. Israel, the country to which Amos let them know, couldn't or would not understand. What a disgrace! There were such huge numbers of different facts about God that the Hebrew people still needed to learn, as well. How might the Hebrews come to know every one of these things?

A Man Who Was Deserted

Despite the fact that Amos had told the people in Israel that Jehovah needed them to obey him, they didn't alter their way of life. Another person would need to convince them on that it should be possible. A man named Hosea was preparing to do only that.

Hosea more likely than not addressed Israel at about a similar time that Amos did. Or on the other hand maybe he carried on an exceptionally brief time after Amos. We can't make certain, for he doesn't let us know. Hosea doesn't reveal to us where he originated from either, however the more likely than not lived in Israel.

In any event, nobody in Israel considered him a foreigner. Hosea doesn't disclose to us what he accomplished professionally. He only educates us regarding an incredible despondency that he had in his life. That is all we have to know, for that was the way Hosea came to become familiar with the most significant truth anybody at any point had found out about God. What was this thing that transpired? What's more, what did he gain from it?

Hosea's significant other had run off and left

him and their three youngsters. That was awful enough, however then Hosea started to find out about other insidious things she was doing. This made Hosea pitiful; it aggravated him as well. How cruelly he would need to punish this runaway spouse when he discovered her!

Hosea found her finally. One day he saw her in the slave market. Yet, now she was a battered hopeless animal. She dislike the delightful woman he had loved. Would it be advisable for him to dismiss and leave her there-just as he never had seen her?

Or on the other hand would it be a good idea for him to hold onto her and punish her? Hosea accomplished none of these things. Rather, he pardoned her and carried her to their home again in light of the fact that he cherished her. This was the manner by which Hosea realized what Jehovah wanted Israel to know.

Run-a-way Israel

Now Hosea saw how Jehovah felt about his people. Israel had broken every one of her vows to Jehovah, similarly as his significant other had broken her vows to him. Israel's wrongdoings (sins) made Jehovah pitiful and irate. Everything about Israel wasn't right; nothing was right. When the Hebrews initially had settled in Canaan, a considerable lot of them had loved Canaan's agnostic divine beings (idol gods). A considerable lot of despite everything them were busy worshiping Baal.

Israel's kings had done nothing to take their people back to Jehovah. Actually, they even had driven their people to adore foreign gods. At that point, as the people became more distant and more distant away from Jehovah, they overlooked increasingly more of his laws. They ransacked, killed, lied, bamboozled everything! What befell the Hebrews' vows to be faithful to Jehovah only and to obey with his laws?

Israel's Terrible Harvest

Hosea thought of the considerable number of times he had watched farmers disperse their seed. At the point when they planted wheat, they realized they would procure wheat at reap time. The people of Israel had "planted" malicious; now they should hope to "harvest" (reap) more prominent underhandedness (greater evil).

Terrible just could prompt more regrettable. Hosea was certain that Israel's bad behavior (sins) just could carry the nation to ruin.

There was no other way out of it. Anyway, Israel didn't merit anything better. Be that as it may, how could affluent, glad Israel be setting out toward ruin? Hosea had a basic response for that. Israel had the right to be decimated by another country. He was similarly as sure that Assyria would do it (Hosea 5:13, 14).

If that was all Hosea had stated, we may never have known about him. Be that as it may, there was something more. Hosea proceeded to enlighten his people with a brilliant truth regarding God that they had to know. Regardless of what they had done, regardless of what they merited, and regardless of what befell them, he stated, Jehovah still loved them and wanted to take them back.

Jehovah's Love

This was the significant thing that Hosea learned in his very own life. His significant other had the right to wind up in the slave market where he discovered her. Be that as it may, Hosea had still loved her and taken her back.

Now he realized that despite the fact that Israel must be pulverized, Jehovah still loved his people and wanted to forgive them and take them back.

It was difficult for the Hebrews to comprehend what Hosea said. They generally had idea that issue came to them just when Jehovah was furious with them. Hosea said this was not true. So he continued informing his people regarding Jehovah's love for them. Jehovah consistently would love them, he stated, in any event, when they were being punished for all their bad behavior (sin).

If anything could have carried Israel's people to change, knowing how much Jehovah loved them ought to have done it. Be that as it may, Israel couldn't or would not comprehend. Maybe just a couple of sincere Hebrews comprehended what Hosea had said.

These Hebrews always remembered his great message, for they recorded it for others to follow. His words would help other people come to learn of God's love. Still it would be quite a while before Jesus could come to let us know, "God is love." For this message, be that as it may, Hosea had helped prepare the world.

Meanwhile, what was to happen to Israel? Israel couldn't love the One who loved them.

Hosea 11:1-9. The entirety of Hosea's message is in this fine poem.

Israel's Last Chance

Trouble was headed to Israel. During all these years, Assyria had been growing stronger and stronger. Now, an eager king called Tiglath-pileser III had become its ruler.

(Who can censure (blame) the Bible storywriters for calling the ruler with this long name "Pul"!) At the leader of his military, Pul came marching toward the west.

From the outset, oddly, Israel was happy for Pul's visit toward the west. Israel's King Menahem wanted Pul to shield him from an old adversary, Syria. Normally, the Assyrian king was happy to step in (II Kings 15:17-22). Pul also was happy to take away the fortune (treasure) that Menahem brought to him (II Kings 15:17-22).

Be that as it may, not long after this, an official in Israel's military army stole the throne from Menahem's sons. This new king Pekah then attempted to win back Israel's freedom from Pul.

As Ahab had done some time before, Pekah now united with Rezin, ruler of Syria. (It appears that a large portion of Syria's kings probably had been named "Rezin"!) Other little nations rushed to help them against the Assyrians.

Israel and Syria wanted king Ahaz of Judah to support them. Ahaz, in any case, wanted to keep out of this. Judah was more distant away from Assyria than Israel was; the South probably won't be disturbed. When Ahaz wouldn't help, Pekah and Rezin chose to show these Judeans some things!

They would make them help. Syria and Israel immediately assembled their armies and marched into Judah. Now, what could Judah do (II Kings 16:5)?

A Different Kind Of Prophet

If at any point Judah's above all else Ahaz had needed a word of wisdom, he did now. Be that as it may, who could give it? What's more, would the king listen at any rate? Ahaz was not the sort of king we could have wanted for Judah to have. He had energized a wide range of baal worship in

Judah. He even had sacrificed his very own child in an ugly agnostic ceremony.

Regardless of whether Ahaz wanted counsel or not, he would get some - from a prophet named Isaiah. Who was Isaiah? From where did he come? Also, what did he need to say?

Isaiah was not a poor worker or shepherd. He more likely than not had a place with one of Judah's imperial (royal) families. Maybe he was a prince, or a priest, or both, for he could walk straight up and converse with the king. Whoever he was, he had sharp eyes that saw everything going on around him.

He saw every one of the wrongs in Judah that Amos and Hosea had found in Israel-tricking to get rich, worshiping foreign gods, and all the rest. Isaiah saw every one of these things and that's just the beginning but at the same time he didn't take care of them. At that point something stunning happened to change his whole life.

A Moment That Changed A Life

Isaiah was worshiping in the Temple in Jerusalem one day. That was when and where it occurred.

Isaiah 6: 1-8. These verses tell of Isaiah's vision in the Temple. This was the means by which he came to know that he should be a prophet and represent Jehovah in Judah.

No big surprise Isaiah trembled. He could consider just how rebellious he and his people were. Only if he could flee! In the event that no one but he could shroud himself! Isaiah was scared almost to death until he realized that Jehovah forgave him. At that point he knew that Jehovah wanted him to speak an exceptional (special) message to his people, What a change that was!

What was the uncommon assignment that Jehovah had for Isaiah? He was to advise Judah to change its ways - similarly as Amos and Hosea had cautioned Israel. He began doing that not long after Hosea had told Israel of Jehovah's love.

An Impossible Task

Inside and out he could consider, Isaiah revealed Jehovah's message to his people. He even composed it into the names of his two sons. He called one son "A Remnant Shall Return." Isaiah implied that there was as yet an opportunity for certain people in Judah to serve Jehovah as they should (Isaiah 7:3).

The other son he called "Swift is the Spoil, Speedy is the Prey." This name makes no difference to us, however it told everybody then that Israel and Syria would be devastated, destroyed very, soon (Isaiah 8:3).

Notwithstanding everything Isaiah did or stated, however, the people would not listen.

A king Who Would Not Listen

Now when Israel and Syria came down to assault Judah, Isaiah went directly to the king. King Ahaz wanted to pay Assyria to secure Judah. Isaiah recognized what that would mean. At the point when word of it got to Egypt, the Pharaoh would send his military into Palestine to drive away the Assyrians.

At that point Judah would be in the center. That could never do. "Resist the urge to panic." Isaiah told the king. "Jehovah will deal with us if we trust in him. Israel and Syria will before long be good and gone (Isaiah 7).

What occurred next more likely than not made Isaiah miserable. Ahaz didn't have the mental fortitude to trust in Jehovah's assurance. Rather, he approached the Assyrian king for help. Tiglath-pileser ("Pul") readily took the Temple treasures that Ahaz sent to him. Consequently, he vowed to support the little Hebrew country. He would save Judah. Be that as it may, Judah would need to continue carrying fortune to him (II Kings 16:5-9).

The Assyrian ruler was absolutely trustworthy. He assaulted Israel - something he would do at any rate - and vanquished all its territory. This was the start of the end for Israel.

This was likewise the start of new issues for Judah. When Ahaz took more fortune to the Assyrian king, he found what else he should do. Ahaz wanted to place another altar in the Temple at Jerusalem - a special altar to the Assyrian king's god!

What a blow that was to the people of Judah. What a significant expense to pay. It would have been something more, a few people in Judah more likely than not suspected, for their country to pay with its life - as Israel did. Time had run out for Israel (II Kings 16:10-18).

Israel's Last Days

Were Amos or Hosea as yet living when the Assyrian armed forces cleared into Israel? We don't have the foggiest idea. This was what they had seen coming.

After the residue (dust) was settled, Israel was saved for a brief period when its new king vowed to serve Pul. In any case, at that point it revolted once more. At that, Assyria new king, Shalmaneser V, and his more stronger armed forces swarmed into Israel. The land was demolished.

Just Samaria, the capital city that Omri and Jeroboam had made into a strong fortification, had the option to wait. In any case, three hard long years of attack were more than even Samaria could take. Finally, battered by the armed forces of Shalmaneser's son, it fell - the last of Israel (II Kings 17:1-6).

The records of Assyria's king above all else disclose to us that Israel's people were removed to far off nations in the East. Just their destroyed land remained. It turned into another country for prisoners that Assyria brought into it from different countries.

The author of our account of the Hebrew

kings was certain since Jehovah had surrendered Israel. In far away Mesopotamia, Israel's people essentially vanished from the pages of history (II Kings 17:7-18). There they became the "Ten Lost Tribes of Israel."

Now only Judah was left to keep the Hebrews' faith in Jehovah alive. Just they were left to reveal God to the remainder of the world. Be that as it may, would Judah be dedicated to Jehovah?

A New Day For Judah

What was going on now in Judah? For quite a long while after Israel was vanquished, better occasions came to Judah. Be that as it may, as usual, inconvenience before long came back once more. At the point when Hezekiah, the son of Ahaz, went to the throne, his people continued encouraging him to request Egypt's assistance and to defy Assyria.

Isaiah had lived unobtrusively in Jerusalem during these years. Now he went to the king once more. He knew that Hezekiah was an astute man and a decent king. Maybe he would listen to better exhortation. "Try not to get tangled up with the Egyptians, "Isaiah said. "Try not to request help of any remote countries. Trust only in Jehovah's help.

Isaiah needed to state this again and again. Each time new issue compromised, the people asked, "Who can help us?" Isaiah consistently replied, "Jehovah will help us. Trust in him. He is the only one upon whom you can depend."

Disregarding everything. Judah and other little countries of Palestine rebeled against Assyria. They were certain Egypt would assist them with turning out to be free once more.

Individually, the countries around Judah tumbled to the Assyrians. At long last Jerusalem itself was disregarded. The Assyrian king, Sennacherib, flaunted that he had Hezekiah written in his city "like a feathered creature (bird) in a cage."

After all the hard battling the Assyrians had done, it without a doubt would have been simple for them to take Judah's capital. Certainly, Sennacherib's incredible armed forces walked up to the very walls of Jerusalem.

"Who can help us now?" the people cried. "There is nobody left to help us." Now, if at any point, Isaiah's trust would be put under a magnifying glass!

"Surrender, people of Jerusalem! Hezekiah always will be unable to save you. Give up now," the Assyrian commander yelled up to the scared Hebrews looking down from the city's walls (II Kings 18:17-35)

"All is lost," the people howled when they heard this. "All is lost," the king howled when he saw the enemy's strength. He was practically prepared to surrender (II Kings 18:37).

Just Isaiah was certain that Jehovah would save Jerusalem. Not really as one bolt would be shot into the city, he said (II Kings 19:5-7).

The journalists of our story about the Hebrew kings reveals to us that this time Hezekiah trusted Isaiah's promise. This time he stood firm, they said. Now, what would happen?

Saved

The following morning, when the people of Jerusalem watched out over the city's walls, the Assyrians were no more. What had happened to Sennacherib's military?

Whatever had occurred, Jerusalem was saved. In the event that Jerusalem had been taken, it would have been the finish of Judah.

It had been a close call. The Hebrew people consistently would recall that they had been saved. What's more, they generally would recollect Isaiah's words, "Trust in Jehovah." But when might they realize what that truly implied?

II Kings 19:35, 36. These refrains are a piece of a long anecdote about the Assyrians' attack of Jerusalem in II Kings 18:13-19:37. The equivalent long story was duplicated by a scribe and added to the book of Isaiah's words, as well. -

Isaiah 36:1-37:37. A lot later, some of it became II Chronicles 32:1-23. These accounts assist us with perceiving how scribes duplicated and recopied stories from age to age. Sennacherib's records reveal to us that he left Jerusalem since Hezekiah sent tribute to him in Nineveh!

Another Chance

Isaiah knew that the people of Judah expected to discover that confiding in Jehovah implied obeying him. He also realized that the country would not have any desire to do that. Judah was an too much like Israel.

Some time or another it would need to be obliterated. However, in any event, when that day came, there still would be trust. Isaiah was certain that a portion of the people would be saved to serve Jehovah. He was certain that if even just a few would be saved, Jehovah still could show himself to the entire world through them.

Isaiah 2:2-4. This is probably the best passage in the whole Old Testament. Would you be able to compose your very own poem that communicates a portion of these thoughts?

Still True Today

When we read the expressions of Amos and Hosea and Isaiah today, we find how forward-thinking their messages are. We nearly overlook that these prophets lived quite a while in the very, very distance past.

There is a valid justification for this, obviously. It is on the grounds that despite everything we have to gain proficiency with every one of the things these prophets said some time in the past. Another prophet's words help us to remember this. "What does Jehovah expect of you," he stated, "however to do equity and to adore thoughtfulness and to walk unassumingly with your God?" God still needs this of us (Micah 6:8).

Chapter Eight

By The Rivers Of Babylon

JERUSALEM HAD A CLOSE call!

The Assyrians had done away from the Hebrews' city, yet they may return again whenever, may be soon. Or on the other hand another adversary may compromise the land.

Israel had experienced a similar sort of tension and dread; at that point it had been obliterated. Presently the ball was in Judah's court to live through questionable years. Would Judah come through them superior to anything Israel had - or more regrettable?

Hezekiah's son was ruler of Judah now. The change was not a decent one. He remade all the land's sanctums (shrines) of Baal. During this present Manasseh's long rule new shrines for Assyria's divine beings (idol gods) were worked in Judah.

Special stepped areas to agnostic divine beings were set up even in the Temple at Jerusalem! The future started to look dark for Judah, once more.

Numerous faithful Hebrews stood up against these horrible wrongs, yet they were slaughtered at Manasseh's orders (II Kings 21:1-16).

Lost And Found

A few years after Manasseh passed on, the future started to look more splendid for Judah. His young grandson, Josiah, became the new ruler. Since the Assyrians were growing feeble, youthful Josiah got an opportunity to take care of his kingdom. The priests of the Temple happily helped him do that. Maybe new Judah would straighten out!

"The temple must be cleaned out!" Josiah ordered. "We should fix some of the ruin our foes have caused." Then something energizing occurred. As the laborers were repairing the Temple, the High Priest found a valuable book (scroll) there. It was the Book of the Law! Rapidly the parchment was brought to the king. Josiah stood by enthusiastically for it to be read to him. What could be written in it?

When Josiah heard its words, he groaned and tore his robe hopelessly. The Book of the Law recounted the harsh demands that Jehovah had made of his people - and it told the dreadful discipline he would send them on them if they rebelled. Josiah saw that his country would need to change, and immediately (II Kings 27:8-13).

Living Up To The Law

"My people must hear these words," Josiah said when he had listened to the entirety of the Law. "Our covenant with Jehovah must be restored." He immediately called together the people of Judah to hear everything written in the Book of the Law. At that point, in a solemn ceremony, he and his people promised that they would be faithful to these laws (II Kings 23:1-3).

Down slammed the symbols and images that the people had been worshiping. Forests of trees where these baals were worshiped were scorched to remains. Their special altars were crushed to pieces. Indeed, even the hallowed place (shrine) of Jehovah at Bethel was crushed! Starting now and into the foreseeable future there would have been only a single altar to Jehovah in all the land.

Sacrifices would be offered only at the Temple in Jerusalem-no place else! Attentive priests, could shield foreign ways from crawling into the peoples' worship of Jehovah. Now the Temple became a higher priority than any time in recent memory.

After the sum total of what had been done, there was something different the people needed to accomplish for Jehovah. The Feast of the Passover must be held. Some time in the past their forefathers had expressed gratefulness for being liberated from Egypt; now Josiah's people offered gratitude for being liberated from different idol gods. They had made their covenant with Jehovah once more!

II Kings 23:21-23. The Passover helped the Hebrews to remember how Jehovah had helped their ancestors escape from Egypt. This part of their ancestors' story probably had been composed only a brief span before Josiah's day, for the Hebrews had not caught wind of the Passover until Josiah read this "book of the law."

Maybe he read a portion of the words of Exodus 11 and 12. Maybe the greater part of the "book of the law" was expounded on at that point. Was Judah progressing nicely finally? Maybe the book of the law had helped Josiah save his nation.

An Old Enemy Falls

The people of Judah had still another motivation to be confident; they heard that Assyria was becoming powerless. A new Babylonia was gradually executing Judah's old adversary. Be that as it may, at that point came word that Nineveh, Assyria's capital, had been decimated.

Judah was free finally! Free from Assyria! Free from foreign gods! What could Judah need to fear now?

Egypt immediately responded to that question for the people of Judah. Its military came walking up from the Nile to assault the new Babylonia. The Pharaoh needed to decimate this new country in the East before it could become sufficiently able to attack Egypt.

At this, Josiah and his military hurried out to stop Egypt's warriors. He needed to support the Babylonians. In any case, little Judah didn't get an opportunity. Josiah was murdered, and his country fell-directly under the control of Egypt (II Kings 23:29, 30).

Now Judah needed to pay overwhelming tribute to the Pharaoh. It additionally needed to acknowledge another king whom the Pharaoh chose. By and by the faithful people in the land needed to watch in despair as this Jehoiakim undid the entirety of Josiah's great work. In came the outside idol gods. Up went the pagan shrines. Also, down, down, went Judah (II Kings 23:34-37).

Was there no real way to keep the country from ruin?

Dead Men Tell No Tales

Indeed, even the prophets in Judah were helping King Jehoiakim push the country over the edge of the bluff. A prophet who was faithful to Jehovah needed to escape to Egypt to save his life. However, even there he was not sheltered.

Jehoiakim's colleagues tailed him, followed him down, took him back to Jerusalem, and put him to death. It was a dangerous business to be a prophet for Jehovah in Judah. Would any other person set out to stand up now (Jeremiah 26:20-23)?

The Man Who Showed
Up At The Temple

There was another person! A man named Jeremiah appeared at the Temple one day. Without a second's pause he expressed the most upsetting words Jerusalem had heard in quite a while.

What caused Jeremiah to make some noise again at such a risky time? Jeremiah's explanation was straightforward and superb and difficult. He cherished Judah as if every one of its people were his very own children, and he knew they were going to obliterate themselves. Jeremiah 7:1-15. The prophet knew that worshiping at the Temple didn't compensate for every one of the wrongs of his people.

They Tried To Silence Him

"Obey Jehovah's laws or die," Jeremiah shouted out. "You believe that worshiping in this Temple will guard you from inconvenience (trouble), however you don't treat your neighbors the way in which Jehovah wants you to."

He continued endlessly, reproving the people for much a bigger number of wrongs than Amos had found in Israel. "You worship foreign gods," he cried, similarly as Hosea had disclosed to Israel quite a while in the past. "You make a wide range of sacrifices and offerings," he stated, "however Jehovah only needs you to obey him and be faithful to him."

At that point Jeremiah said the most horrendous thing of all. "In the event that you go on like this," he stated, "this land will turn into a desert, and any person who needs to stay here in it will wish he were dead!"

"Wish he were dead!" resounded the priests and the king's manikin prophets. "Okay. We'll deal with that for you at the present time," they cried. They held onto Jeremiah.

Rapidly they sent to the king's castle for the princes to come and hold court. It would be a quick preliminary, a definite sentence of death, and an expedient end for one more troublemaker (Jeremiah 26:7-11).

Don't Say It – Write It

Shockingly, Jeremiah was sent away from the Temple alive. He always would be unable to go there once more. The princes had ordered him to be warded off by force, if necessary. How could his message ever be heard there again? He never could push his way past the imposing watchmen who were there to keep him out (Jeremiah 26:12).

The prophet found a way. It was simple, yet it likewise was perilous. Baruch, Jeremiah's unwavering scribe, composed his message on a parchment (scroll). At that point Baruch went to the Temple and read Jeremiah's words! This time the message was much more awful than previously. It likewise made the king angrier than it had previously (Jeremiah 36:1-19).

"Our country must be eager to serve Babylonia," Jeremiah had stated, "or Jehovah will bring Babylonia's chariots down on Jerusalem like a tornado, in view of Judah's wickedness."

Jeremiah 4:13-18. Everybody knew that Jeremiah was talking about Babylonia, since he talked about peril originating from the heading of Dan and Mount Ephraim. Jeremiah's words are a poem in the Hebrew language.

Baruch or another person who heard him talk probably put his words into poetry. Poems could be recalled and rehashed all the more effectively. That most likely is the reason a significant number of the words of Amos and Hosea and Isaiah are poems.

Write It Again

Jehoiakim didn't care for this by any stretch of the imagination. The Egyptians had made him Judah's king. He liked things to remain as such.

Now it was the king's time to act. He had Jeremiah's parchment (scroll) brought to him at his royal residence. As one section after one more of the prophet's message was read, the king himself cut it from the scroll with a blade and put it in the fire (Jeremiah 36:20-26).

Now the ball was in Jeremiah's court once more. He was disheartened, however he would not surrender. Baruch had kept in touch with one parchment (scroll); he could compose another. Along these lines, for a subsequent time, Jeremiah gradually rehashed the entirety of Jehovah's message while Baruch recorded the horrible words. This was something that Jehovah needed to say. It must be said. What's more, it needed to remain said! Be that as it may, would Judah listen (Jeremiah 36:27-32)?

A New Master Over Judah

Egypt's rule over Judah didn't last any longer. The Babylonians prevailed upon an incredible triumph over Egypt in a seething fight at Carchemish, far north of Judah. That was the end of Egypt as a great power. Be that as it may, it didn't make Judah free. Now Judah needed to pay tribute to King Nebuchadnezzar of Babylonia.

As a matter of fact, Judah was in a more awful spot than any time in recent memory. Egypt, despite the fact that it had been beaten, now attempted to get Judah to oppose Babylonia. That could just bring issue maybe even obliteration. How could this country be saved with the goal that it could in any case be used by God?

Jeremiah attempted to shield Judah from opposing Babylonia, yet futile. At the point when Babylonia's military nearly was beaten in an assault on Egypt. Jehoiakim thought he saw his opportunity to be free once more.

He revolted. Yet, before poor, moronic Jehoiakim could state "Nebuchadnezzar," there He was, his armies and all.

Jerusalem was encompassed. Jehoiakim died. His son Jehoiachin surrendered himself to save the city. King Nebuchadnezzar reclaimed to Babylonia every one of the people of Judah who could be of any use to him.

He additionally removed the entirety of the princes and strict loaders; these work up inconvenience whenever left behind. Everything of worth was taken from the royal residence, the Temple, and the homes of the city, Jerusalem was a phantom town, yet at any rate regardless it was standing. This had been another close escape!

Jeremiah's heart hurt for the hostages who had been removed. In any case, what might he be able to do now? He could reveal to them the great thing about Jehovah that he had learned. So Jeremiah composed a letter to them (Jeremiah 29:4-14).

Jeremiah needed the outcasts to realize that Jehovah was with them and would hear their prayers in Babylonia.

The Last King

Nebuchadnezzar put a new king on the throne in Judah. He thought he had picked somebody who might be faithful to him. In any case, this Zedekiah couldn't be depended on. First he would listen to Jeremiah who cautioned him, "Obey Nebuchadnezzar; Jehovah wants this." Then he would listen to other people who said, "Make a plot with Egypt; defy Babylonia."

Jeremiah had spoken; he had composed; now he showcased the message Jehovah wanted Judah to hear. It was a bizarre sight to see the prophet wearing a burden around his neck (a yoke), however what he was stating by it was clear. Judah must serve Nebuchadnezzar, or the end would come to them all of a sudden and unquestionably.

This was also consistent with Zedekiah to go along with them and radical against Babylonia. "Jehovah, the God who made all the earth and everything in it, has made you servants of Nebuchadnezzar," Jeremiah told their envoys (Jeremiah 27:1-17).

In any case, the prophet couldn't convince either his own king or these rogues from different nations. They had come to Jerusalem to plot an insubordination, and the king was eager to get together with them. Finally, Judah revolted.

When The End Came

Nebuchadnezzar's Babylonian soldiers encompassed Jerusalem once more. The people paused. Would something happen to save them as it had in the times of Hezekiah? Most likely Jehovah would save them, the people of Jerusalem thought. They recalled that Isaiah had stated, "Trust in Jehovah." Jeremiah, however, continued saying, "Surrender," (or give up)!

The people of Jerusalem would not surrender. They trusted that the Egyptians would protect them. Months passed by. Food supplies fell lower and lower. Be that as it may, the city still waited. When king Zedekiah at long last surrendered hope, he and a portion of his men attempted to get away. That was miserable. They just fell under the control of the Babylonians-to confront coldblooded torment and death.

It took just about two years for the Babylonians to pound through Jerusalem's walls, however this time the decimation was completed. Everything important was diverted from the Temple. The Babylonians put a match to the once-sublime structure. The entire city was burned. Indeed, even the walls were battered down.

"Jerusalem never will rise again," said the Babylonian officers gladly, as they took a look at their work.

"We never will see our homes again," said the people as they glanced back at the vestiges. With the exception of a rare sorts of people who got away to Egypt, they would experience their days in Babylonia (II Kings 24:20b-25:26).

It was 587 B.C. The kingdom of Judah had died.

An End-Or A New Beginning?

The starved, startled prisoners who thought back on the flaring vestiges of Jerusalem never would overlook the sight. They never would overlook the suffering they had experienced there - pausing, pausing, trusting that the city will fall. Be that as it may, now they confronted something surprisingly more terrible as prisoners.

What number would have the option to live through the moderate, murdering walk to a weird land far away in the East? It would be hard enough for resilient men with strong bodies to walk 600 miles over stones and thistles.

How could the starved hostages and particularly the women and children and more older persons oversee? The sun would pound on them in the daytime; they would shudder in the harsh cold of the evenings.

'Maybe it would have been exceptional to bite the dust in the remains than to endure the long, long days and evenings that lay in front of them now. Also, what was waiting for them toward the end of their walk?

The hostages more likely than not recollected accounts of how their ancestors had been dealt with quite a while in the past when they were in Egypt. "We will be slaves everlastingly," they probably thought. "Jehovah won't save his people again."

Surprise In A New Land

The a huge number of hostages who came securely to Babylonia found another sort of life waiting for them there. With the exception of one spot that is notice in the Bible, we don't have the foggiest idea where the prisoners were settled. This "River Chebar" was an incredible channel close to the city of Nippur.

Any place they settled, they by and by were in the land where their history had started - back in the place that is known for Abraham. Every one of the urban areas probably been especially similar to the fine city at Ur that he had known hundreds of years prior.

Incredibly, the prisoners were very well treated in Babylonia. They didn't need to live as hopeless slaves. They even were permitted to live respectively in gatherings of their own. They could construct houses, plant cultivates, and have workers of their own.

They even could start a new business for themselves. Actually, when the Hebrew prisoners lost their dread, they found that life is wealthy in this rich land was superior to anything it had been in Palestine. Here the farms flourished. The grand sanctuaries of Babylonia's gods caused the Temple of Jerusalem to appear to be little and poor.

Forgetting And Learning

However, the Hebrews couldn't overlook their old home where Jehovah's Temple had been in Jerusalem. That was Jehovah's land. That was the place he should be worshiped. "How might we worship Jehovah here?" the outcasts pondered. In any case, might anyone be able to accuse these outcasts in the event that they overlooked their country and even Jehovah in this new land?

A portion of the outcasts before long forgot. They became "Babylonians" themselves. In any case, others remembered their ties with the past. Their trust in Jehovah didn't bite the dust; it even started to live as it never had lived in Judah! In this way, rather than getting lost among every one of the people of Babylonia, these outcasts grew closer to Jehovah and to each other.

The best part is that they came to become familiar with a portion of the significant facts about God that they had expected to learn. In Babylonia they discovered that they didn't need to be in the Temple at Jerusalem to worship Jehovah. Now the Hebrew people figured out how to say, "Our Temple might be in ruins, but Jehovah hears us when we go to him here."

Now the people comprehended what Jeremiah implied when he had said that Jehovah would place his law in their hearts. Now they came to comprehend that every last one of them could know and trust in Jehovah for himself.

"It's not possible for anyone to find out about Jehovah for you," Jeremiah had said. "It's not possible for anyone to trust in Jehovah for you.

Every person must do that for himself. In any case, he wants you to know him, and he will help you with trusting him."

Jeremiah 31:31-34. The Hebrew people had believed that Jehovah could be worshiped only in their land at the Temple in Jerusalem since he was their nation's god. Jeremiah helped them discover that anybody could worship Jehovah anyplace, and that each person must trust in Jehovah for himself.

A New Voice In Babylonia

How the outcasts more likely than not wanted that Jeremiah were with them now. Be that as it may, he had remained in Jerusalem. Maybe the outcasts in Babylonia never knew until years after the fact what had happened to Jeremiah.

A gathering of Hebrews who got away to Egypt had constrained the old prophet to go there with them. There he died - maybe he was murdered there-far away from the city he had loved and attempted to save (Jeremiah 43:1-7).

Now, there were other prophets to address the Hebrew people. One of these was a man named Ezekiel. He had been taken to Babylonia with the youthful King Jehoiachin. Ezekiel also helped the Hebrews know that Jehovah cared about every person in their nation.

Ezekiel 18:1-4, 19,20, 30-32. Ezekiel helped the Hebrews discover that each person was liable for his own actions, not for what his country or any other person had done. The last verses helped the Hebrews discover that Jehovah wanted to forgive each person no matter what wrongs he had done.

A New Life in Babylonia

Ezekiel also helped the outcasts learn how to worship Jehovah in new ways. In Babylonia they started to get together in little gatherings to worship on the Sabbath. They couldn't offer sacrifices without their Temple, but they could say prayers and sing the psalms that they once had sung there.

They could tell again and again the narratives of their ancestors. They could consider the lessons of the prophets. They could study Jehovah's Law or "Torah" and consider what it implied. The Sabbath came to mean more to the Hebrews now than it had at any point implied previously.

Rather than overlooking their past, the outcasts recollected that it like never before. Even better, they likewise recorded it. The narratives and the lessons of the Hebrew people that had been passed along for such a large number of ages were recorded finally.

Records that had been written down before were composed over in new ways. A considerable amount of the books of the Old Testament were composed during these years when the Hebrews lived in Babylonia.

A New Name

During these years, the people came to be known by another name. When they had been called Hebrews; at that point they had come to be called Israelites for some time. At the point when Israel in the north and Judah in the south became two separate countries once more, the people had been called Israelites and Judeans.

After Israel fell, only Judah was left. Presently, the Judeans in Babylonia came to be known as Jews. These Jews were the remainder of Jehovah's special people. They now were the people who must show him to his world.

New Questions – New Answers

The Jews became used to living in Babylonia. Their life there turned out to be better constantly. Numerous inquiries still beset them.

The people asked, "Has Jehovah overlooked (forgotten) us? Doesn't he care what befalls us any longer?" They had heard enough about their past and the defiance of their people. They knew they had the right to live in a state of banishment. In any case, was there no forgiveness for them, ever?

When the Jews started to ask themselves these new inquiries, God could disclose to them something he generally had wanted them to know. God's message came to them now through the words of a prophet whose name we never will know. Maybe and, after its all said and done nobody truly knew who composed these delightful poems that we read in our Bible today.

Isaiah 40:1-5, 11. "Jehovah has pardoned you. Be comforted," the prophet's message said. "He is watching over you like a shepherd."

The people still pondered. "What is to happen to us now?" they inquired. "Will we stay away for the indefinite future to our homeland?"

Isaiah 45:1-6. "Jehovah has chosen someone

who does not even know him to deliver us," the prophet replied. "Cyrus the Persian will deliver us from Babylonia, because Jehovah is ready for us to go home, now."

Could this be true? Truly, it is valid, the prophet stated, on the grounds that Jehovah had a special mission for them. This was something that Jehovah consistently had wanted of them. Now they would be ready to do it for him.

Isaiah 42:5-8. "Jehovah wants us to help all of the people of the world to know he is the only God. He wants us to help them know that he is their God, as well, and that he cares about them. Then they will know that they had thought their gods had done for them."

Had Jehovah truly chose them, the Jews, to inform all the world concerning him? Now, the Jews started to know why they generally had been Jehovah's people and how they should serve him.

A Bridge To The New Testament

How strange it is that we don't have a clue about this current prophet's name! All we know is that his compositions came to be added to the book of Isaiah. This once led many people to accept that Isaiah of Jerusalem had verbally expressed these words to the people of Babylon.

However, today we know that the words we read in Isaiah 40-66 couldn't have been composed by him. So we have come to consider this prophet the "Second Isaiah." The "first" Isaiah had addressed the people of Jerusalem quite a while in the past. This prophet addressed the Jews in Babylonia, right around 200 years after the fact.

We consider Second Isaiah as the best of all the Old Testament prophets. There is an extraordinary purpose behind this. He fabricates a kind of scaffold (bridge) between the Old Testament and the New Testament.

His words make us consider Jesus, for Jesus served God similarly as Second Isaiah had said that Jehovah wanted the Jews to serve him. To get this, however, you should read his words for yourself.

Isaiah 53:3-6. The Jews were to be Jehovah's servant nation for the sake of everyone in the world. It would not be easy. They would face a much suffering when others did wrong. But this would help other people to come to know how much Jehovah loved them and wanted them to serve him.

Why do these words make you think of Jesus?

A Second Exodus

The Jews' stay in Babylonia was to end very soon. Babylonia had been a subsequent Egypt. Before long they would return to the Promised Land once more. When they left Babylonia, would they be prepared finally to do their special mission for God?

Chapter Nine

Home Again

TIME WAS RUNNING OUT for the Babylonian Empire. It didn't have long to go. At that point it would fall, similarly as it had made other empires fall.

Babylonia was not a strong country any more. As far back as Nebuchadnezzar's time, the nation had lost increasingly more of its power. While Babylonia was becoming feeble, the Persians, who lived in the lands east of Babylonia, were becoming strong.

When Cyrus, king of Persia, brought his military marching up to the strong gates of Babylon in 539 B.C., the city didn't set up a battle (start a fight). Truth be told, it opened its doors to him. The Babylonians respected this strong, new king from the East. The Jews considered him a deliverer.

A Dream Come True

In a day when one conqueror or ruler was a coldblooded as the following, Cyrus was unique. He didn't crush urban areas and take their fortunes. He didn't send vanquished people from their homes to faraway lands.

Actually, he even wanted the hostages in Babylonia to come back to their old countries. There they should use their very own language, pursue their own traditions, and love their own gods. Cyrus' delivery people (messengers) were sent to Babylonia to carry this uplifting news to the people.

How the Jews probably rushed to where the king's declaration would have been read! Amazingly, the envoy even read the king's words in the language they knew.

The king's flag-bearer didn't address them in Persian, however in Aramaic. This language, which was particularly similar to Hebrew, was the language that the Jews currently were utilizing in regular day to day life.

Ezra 1:2-4. In his engraving on the renowned "Cyrus Cylinder," King Cyrus reveals to us that Marduk, the god of the land, had helped him.

The Old Testament essayist of these verses was certain that Jehovah truly had helped Cyrus, so in his story he reveals to us this is the thing that Cyrus said.

The Jews could barely believe their ears. The Temple at Jerusalem was to be rebuilt- right where Solomon's Temple had stood!

The king would give the Jews enough cash to pay for the work. All the valuable vessels and Temple decorations that had been brought by Nebuchadnezzar to Babylonia were to be returned (II Chronicles 36:22, 23; Ezra 1:1-4).

A Few Return

Not long after Cyrus promised these things to the Jews, he selected a leader to assist them with beginning. Cyrus' decision for their leader more likely than not made the Jews happy. He was a youthful Jewish ruler named Sheshbazzar. This youthful ruler was a son of Jehoiachin, the king whom Nebuchadnezzar had brought to Babylon as a hostage (Ezra 1:5-11).

The Jews wanted to return to Jerusalem to revamp the Temple. They had been anticipating that as far back as they had been brought to

Babylonia. However, when Sheshbazzar set out for their old country, only a few of the outcasts (exiles) went with him. How could this be?

There were a few reasons. The Jews had lived in Babylonia quite a while. Fifty years had gone since the last outcasts had come there from Jerusalem. Only a few really remembered their country - and they, obviously, were old.

The more youthful Jews had heard their fathers tell how their country had been destroyed. "What is there to come back to?" they inquired. "For what reason would it be advisable for us to surrender our agreeable life here in Babylonia for that?"

It more likely than not appeared to be stupid to consider beginning on a long, hard voyage - and only to live in a poor, demolished city! Some may go later, but now they would trust that others will get the hardest part of the activity done! Others didn't even care whether the Temple was remade or not! So just a valiant few came back to remake their demolished Temple and homeland.

The people who went with Sheshbazzar started to establish the framework of the Temple, but that was all. They scarcely survived a long dry season. They had no cash in any event, for nourishment (food). It was no big surprise that their work reached a stand-still. It appeared that the Temple could never be revamped. Would they forget Jehovah - and his mission for them (Ezra 5:16)?

The House Of The Lord

A few years after the fact, another Jewish prince became legislative (governor) leader of Judah. This new representative, Zerubbabel, supported the Jews in Jerusalem. They initially fabricated an altar for their penances. At that point the establishment for the new Temple before long was done. This was their first achievement (Ezra 3:2-9).

How the developers celebrated when the last stone of the establishment was laid. There was glad singing. Be that as it may, there was sobbing, as well. "It won't resemble Solomon's Temple," some shattered old people wailed (sobbed). A few of the outcasts still remembered that glorious Temple. Did they remember their people's mission for Jehovah (Ezra 3:10-13).

Trouble From Neighbors

They had caused a fine start, to however even Zerubbabel could do no more. The Jews had neighbors in Judah who didn't want the Temple to be done. These neighbors were inconvenient "outsiders" (foreigners) who had been brought into Palestine when Judah's people had been taken from their country.

"What will befall us?" these people pondered. "In the event that the Jews reconstruct their Temple, they will need to guarantee their old urban areas once more, as well. Increasingly more of them will return to live here. That would be awful for us." So these people did whatever they could to shield the new Temple from being completed. They had come to view Judah as their territory.

In spite of the fact that the people around Jerusalem didn't want the Temple to be built, Judah's neighbors toward the north did. Some time in the past Israel's ten tribes had lived there - until their country fell. At that point the Assyrians had carried new people into the district around Samaria to supplant the banished Hebrews. A wide range of issue had happened to these new pioneers.

Hence, they had started to worship Jehovah. They had been certain that issues had come to them since they were not worshiping the gods of the land! Now, after very nearly 200 years, these Samaritans were satisfied that there would have been a fine new Temple for Jehovah in Jerusalem. They would help build it and come there to worship (II Kings 17:14-28).

This Is Our Temple

The Samaritans sent envoys to Jerusalem to disclose to Zerubbabel that they were the Jews' companions. "Give us a chance to work with you," the Samaritans stated, "for we have worshiped the God of Israel as far back as we have come to this land."

Zerubbabel took a look at his enthusiastic guests with disdain (scorn). "We don't need your assistance, "he replied. "This is our Temple!" for goodness' sake! What did this mean?

The Jews didn't consider the Samaritans sufficient or good enough to assist them with building their Temple to Jehovah. "The

Samaritans' religion is stirred up with agnostic religion (pagan religion)," they said. "So we can't bear to get mixed up with them!"

After this, the Samaritans did everything they could to keep the Jews from building the Temple. They had been offended; now they were furious and insulted. They composed a letter to the Persian king; in it they blamed the Jews for plotting to revolt. That brought the work in Jerusalem to a stop. Meanwhile, Samaritans set up a sanctuary (temple) of their won on Mt. Gerizim (Ezra 4:4-24)!

Somewhat later, two prophets, Haggai and Zechariah, urged the people to take a stab at remaking the Temple once more. At last, it was completed (Ezra 5:1-2; 6:13-18). It was not as lovely or as huge as Solomon's Temple had been, but it was a dream worked out. It was an indication of Jehovah's presence among his people.

One day this new Temple was dedicated. It was a glorious day for the people who had returned to their old homeland. Now maybe, these people would be ready for God to use them to demonstrate his ways to all the world.

Let Us Rise Up And Build

Now in history of the Jews, there are many missing "pages." We can't get our story again until around seventy years after the Temple was dedicated. What occurred during these "missing years"?

Did the Jews go directly on reconstructing the city of Jerusalem? The books of Nehemiah and Ezra assist us with filling in a portion of the holes, yet we may never have answers to the entirety of our inquiries. Maybe the story of the Jews starts again with a report that came to Persia from Judah.

Things were not going admirably in Jerusalem, the report said. Updates on the disintegrated walls of the old Hebrew capital by one way or another had gotten right to Susa, the Persian ruler's winter capital.

The miserable news went to a man named Nehemiah, a relative of the Jewish outcasts in Babylonia. It couldn't have gone to a superior man. Nehemiah had become the confided in cup-bearer to the Persian king (Nehemiah 1)

Nehemiah was dismal when he caught wind of the wretchedness of his people in Jerusalem.

At the point when the Persian king discovered the explanation behind Nehemiah's distress, he vowed to help the battling Jews in Jerusalem rebuild their city (Nehemiah 2:1-8).

The king delegated Nehemiah legislative head (or governor) of Judah. At that point he did considerably more! He composed a letter to the attendant of his woodland. It stated, "Let Nehemiah have as a lot of timber as he needs to use to remake the walls and gates of Jerusalem." No one could have requested much else!

The Walls and Gates Of Jerusalem

Nehemiah set out on the long road to Jerusalem with high expectations. At Jerusalem, he found that things were more regrettable than he had suspected. One night he made a mystery voyage through the walls. Fixes were required all over the place. No big surprise the people in the messed up city dreaded the enemies surrounding them (Nehemiah 2:11-20).

The walls of the city must be remade before whatever else. The work was begun. In any case, at that point Jerusalem's neighbors started to raise hell, similarly as they had when the Temple was being constructed. This disheartened the developers (Nehemiah 4:6-9).

Fortunately, Nehemiah thought of an approach to outmaneuver his people's foes. How the people functioned; at that point incredibly, the walls that had been in ruin for in excess of a hundred years were assembled again in around forty days!

How the people celebrated and sang on the day that the walls were dedicated. They had their homes in Jerusalem once more. They had their Temple once more. Also, now, at long last, their city was sheltered inside its own walls once more. What more could a people need!

Nehemiah realized that the people required something more than the solid walls of the city around them. They needed to become strong in their loyalty to Jehovah, their God, the only God of all the earth.

Something must be done to shield them from following the agnostic ways of their neighbors. Something must be done to cause them to comply with the Jewish law, the Torah.

Many, numerous Jewish men had hitched "outside" spouses. In some cases their children didn't learn how to speak Hebrew and didn't study the Jewish laws - the Torah. The people were purchasing and selling and carrying on business on the Sabbath. How might he make the people honor the Sabbath as they should?

Help was en route. A priest named Ezra was originating from Babylon to help the people of Judah learn and comply with the laws of their religion.

Rebuilding Judah's Life

Ezra didn't come to be a governor as Nehemiah had been. Ezra came to be a religious leader of the Jews in Judah and particularly in Jerusalem. He had gotten consent from the Persian king to go to Jerusalem with a parade of returning outcasts (exiles).

The first exiles had come back to Jerusalem very nearly a hundred years prior. Other little trains of Jews had pursued every now and then from that point forward. At this point, Jerusalem truly had become a decent place to live in once more.

These returning outcasts (exiles) carried with them a little fortune of silver and gold for the Temple in Jerusalem. The most significant thing in Ezra's baggage, was a duplicate of the book of the law - the Torah (Ezra 7:1-10).

Ezra found that life in Jerusalem was more terrible than he had dreaded. The people knew no more about Jehovah's laws than they had in Josiah's day - before the scroll of the law had been found in the Temple. The messages of the prophets had been forgotten.

These people wanted to make the right choice. They knew that they were not living by Jehovah's laws. So they solicited Ezra to bring the scroll from the book of the law to the public square and to read it to them.

Listening To The Law

Promptly in the first part of the day (early morning) one day Ezra started reading the words of the law to the people. He read endlessly until early afternoon. Assistants held on, clarifying the laws that the people didn't comprehend. At that point, in the days that observed, the law was read to the people several more times.

It was perused again during the seven-day Feast of Tabernacles. This was an extraordinary celebration that helped the Jews to remember how their ancestors had come into Canaan in the times of Joshua, long, long, ago (Nehemiah 8).

Toward the end of this Feast of Tabernacles, the people seriously made a covenant with Jehovah once more. In a long discourse, Ezra helped the people to remember all that Jehovah had accomplished for them.

They vowed to comply with his laws, similarly as the Hebrews had done quite a while in the past in the times of Moses, and of Joshua, and of Josiah. Now maybe they would be prepared to assist the world to come to know God (Nehemiah 9-10).

Ezra had helped the Jews become certain about something critical to them. He had helped them know that in one significant way they were not the same as every other person in the earth, they were different from others.

They were diverse on the grounds that solitary they knew Jehovah and knew that he was the only true God of all the earth. Now, clearly, they should be prepared to enable all the earth to come to know and to worship him.

A Wall Around The People

Ezra, however, only wanted to ensure their Jewish religion and laws would not be changed by pariahs (outsiders). Nehemiah had helped the people build a strong wall around their city to shield their homes from pariahs. Ezra wanted to build a wall around their religion. How should that be possible?

As Ezra considered this, he turned out to be certain that he should prevent Jews from wedding outside spouses. So that is the thing that he demanded - no more relationships among Jews and pariahs. In any case, that was insufficient for him. He also ordered the men that already was married to foreign women to surrender their wives and families. These wives and their children must be sent away!

We don't have the foggiest idea what occurred after this, for the Book of Ezra closes there. We can only envision what despondency this order more likely than not caused.

The vast majority of all, we need to think about what had befallen the teachings of the unknown prophet whom we call the Second Isaiah. Definitely his teachings ought to have made the Jews want to have everybody know and serve Jehovah with them.

Had these special people previously forgotten the most significant thing they at any point had learned? Maybe that is the thing that consistently happens when suffering and tough times are past.

Laws, Laws, Laws

Ezra told the people that their lives must be guided by Jehovah's laws. That ought to have been something to be thankful for. Be that as it may, at that point the Jews started to include new laws about each and every thing they did.

Their favorite songs told how they thought every Jew should live - "his delight is in the law of the Lord, and on his law he meditates day and night" (Psalm 1).

Had they disregarded Amos' message? Is it safe to say that it was progressively critical to pray and make the numerous sacrifices that their laws demanded - or to do good things for their neighbors?

Had they disregarded Hosea's message? Is it accurate to say that it was increasingly critical to know all that Jehovah demanded of them - or to know how much he loved them and how much he wanted them to love and serve him?

Had they overlooked Isaiah's message? Is it accurate to say that it was increasingly critical to comply with every one of their standards - or to trust in Jehovah's way for them and follow it?

Also, had the people overlooked the Second Isaiah's message? Had they overlooked that Jehovah wanted them to enlighten different countries regarding him with the goal that they would come to serve him?

Prophets Of Hate-And Hope

As the Jews invested more energy and harder to keep themselves separated from different countries, they grew to disdain (dislike) all others. There even were times when their abhorrence developed into contempt. We can see this when we read the Book of Obadiah.

As we read his words, we get an image of this man shaking his finger at the people of near by Edom. "You are going to get what you deserve," he tells them, "and believe me, I'm not sorry!" Why was this (Obadiah 1-4)?

Once, quite a while in the past, Judah had been

friendly with this country. Be that as it may, when Jerusalem tumbled to Nebuchadnezzar, Edom had dismissed fleeing Hebrew outcasts. At that point, to exacerbate the situation, the Edomites had grabbed influence a portion of Judah's land.

Now in Obadiah's time, the tables were turned. Edom was being attacked. At the point when we go to Obadiah's words in the Old Testament, we wonder if the people in Judah at any point will become God's servant nation to show God to the world.

Was Obadiah representing all the Jewish people when he boasted over Edom's issues? Or then again were there people in Judah who felt different (10-18)?

A Prophet Who Tried To Run Away

Fortunately, not every person in Judah felt about different countries as Obadiah did. More than one voice revolted against such terrible sentiments toward outcasts. More than one person said to the people, "We should inform different countries that Jehovah cares concerning them." Some people in Judah were recalling the Second Isaiah message!

One obscure essayist was stressed over this detest in his people. So he composed a story to give them how wrong this was and what Jehovah truly wanted of them. This was exactly what Jesus would do.

At the point when he advised parables to help people comprehend what God wanted of them. Maybe that way the author could cause his people to see that it was so off-base to detest pariahs.

His story was about a prophet named Jonah. Toward the start of his story, this essayist told how Jonah abhorred pariahs. Jonah was extremely, disturbed when Jehovah instructed him to proceed to tell the people of Nineveh that they should change their lifestyle or be demolished. Nineveh was the capital city of the loathed Assyrians of Jeroboam's day!

"What! Help save Nineveh!" Jonah thought. "The Assyrians have been pitiless to my people. I won't help save our adversaries. They should be annihilated."

Jonah attempted to flee from Jehovah and his errand. He fled west to the seaport of Joppa. There he jumped on a vessel for Tarshish, which was close to what we today call Gibraltar. He wanted to get as far away from Nineveh as he could. In any case, Jehovah would not give Jonah a chance to flee.

It resembled the end for Jonah when he was tossed over the edge for bringing alleged misfortune to the ship - similarly as it had resembled the end for Judah when Jerusalem tumbled to Nebuchadnezzar!

In any case, that, as well, was just the start. The essayist of this story told how an "extraordinary fish" took Jonah back to land, free from any danger yet exceptionally troubled! Now Jonah realized that he couldn't flee from Jehovah. Thus he went to Nineveh. The author wanted to make it extremely evident that Jehovah would not give his people a chance to escape doing what he wanted them to do (Jonah 1:1-3:3).

"They won't hear me out," Jonah continued letting himself know in Nineveh. Be that as it may, he wasn't right! The detested Assyrian people started to repent. Before long the entire city changed - even the king! It would resemble that with the entirety of Judah's neighbors. Our essayist was telling his people (3:5-10).

The author proceeded to tell how miserable Jonah was with the consequences of his proclaiming! "It simply wasn't right," he continued speculation, "for Nineveh to be saved."

It was too difficult to even consider believing that Jehovah's affection and forgiving were implied, for the Jews alone, yet for everybody! The author of the Book of Jonah realized that it would be difficult for his people to gain proficiency with this.

Would the Jewish people ever learn how to become God's light to other countries? Would they ever enlighten them regarding God's love for every one of the people of the earth? A few hundred years more would have to pass before this could be.

New Masters For Old

During these next hundreds of years, new domains developed in control, governed for some time, and afterward fell, similarly as they generally had.

The Persian Empire reached a conclusion after around 200 years of administering the terrains of the Fertile Crescent. At that point another vanquisher, Alexander the Great, dominated.

This new leader of all the world had been

educated by a well known Greek educator. He had been such a decent student, that he needed every one of the nations he vanquished to follow the Greek perspective and living.

Alexander's Greek method for living even crawled into Palestine. The Jews who were devoted to their own specific ways of doing things felt this was hazardous. "We will lose our religion," they said. So they made their laws stricter than any time in recent memory and even included new rules for the Jews to follow!

When Alexander the Great died, his tremendous empire was parted into four sections. For some time Palestine was controlled by the Egyptians, then, at some point by the Syrians. During Syria's rule things went more gravely for the Jews than they had since the fall of Jerusalem.

One of Syria's rulers nearly decimated the Jews' religion. He gave orders to prohibit the Jewish religion, the Torah, and all the Jewish functions of worship. He relinquished to his very own agnostic god in the Temple of Jerusalem.

Many Jews yielded to this Syrian kings' orders, yet the bolder ones announced, "We won't let our religion be cleared out at this point. We should be allowed to worship Jehovah."

Messages Of Hope

During these long periods of persecution, a few of the steadfast Jews found another approach to help their people stay loyal. Letters and messages that could be perused furtively started to show up out of the blue. These messages told how Jews had been dedicated during horrendous abuse long, quite a while in the past.

Since these unusual messages not even once said anything regarding the loathed Syrians, the Syrian governors would not have stressed over them regardless of whether they had found them. Be that as it may, the Jews who read these messages knew what they truly implied.

Some unknown Jewish scholars were disclosing to them that Jehovah would help them with winning their freedom from the Syrians in the event that they would be faithful to him.

The Book of Daniel in our Old Testament was one of these messages with a mystery meaning. It told how Daniel stayed consistent with Jehovah regardless of everything that was done to him.

These accounts helped the Jews stay faithful through the most exceedingly awful mistreatment in the entirety of their history. They additionally helped give the Jews boldness to ascend against their Syrian bosses. At the point when all was good and well, they revolted. To their very own amazement, they won! Syria had to release Palestine!

For around a hundred years the Jews were a free country once more. However, they were not ready to stay free. A strong new empire was growing up surrounding them. Before long Palestine was eaten up once more. Judah's new victors were the Romans.

Judea's Last Master-Rome

With its new Roman victors, Judah got another Roman name. Now the land was called Judea, "the place that is known for the Jews." The Romans made some hard memories understanding these people in Judea.

In spite of the fact that they all were Jews, they all were not the same. They were isolated into a few unique groups or gatherings. The poor Romans made some hard memories becoming acquainted with what's in store from every last one of these groups.

Dr. John Thomas Wylie

The Romans' Friends

The Romans didn't have numerous companions among the Jews, however there were a few people in Judea who coexisted well with them. These were the Sadducees. The Romans could comprehend these individuals. The best part is that for the Sadducees helped them rule the nation and gather charges.

The Sadducees were loathed and scorned as double crossers by their own people. To exacerbate the situation, they were the wealthiest people in the land. Since they were affluent, they had the option to purchase unique favors from the Roman governors. They were well off in light of the fact that they helped the Romans.

That was the means by which a Sadducee turned out to be High Priest of the Jews. That made different Jews detest the Romans and the Sadducees and the tax authorities (tax collectors) and the Temple priests all simultaneously. They were all indistinguishable!

Be that as it may, the Sadducees were not stressed. "The best thing for us and for our nation is to oblige the Romans," they continued saying. "We will keep on great terms with them and simultaneously comply with our Jewish laws." "Yet, you don't keep the laws," the Pharisees fought back at them. "You just keep the Torah, the law of Moses.

Furthermore, how might you comply with the Torah that you don't likewise comply with the various laws of our religion? These different laws disclose to you how to comply with the Torah!"

The Lawkeepers Of Judea

These Pharisees never would coexist with the Sadducees. The Sadducees would have nothing to do with the many, numerous strict laws that the Pharisees had added to the old law of Moses.

At the point when a Pharisee said "keep the law," he implied every one of these laws as well - and these laws had been growing up from the hour of Neheniah and Ezra and from that point forward. To the entirety of this the Sadducees derisively stated, "Waste!" No big surprise they didn't get along.

Be that as it may, regardless of when the Sadducees thought, the Pharisees went to any length to keep every one of their laws. Jehovah would compensate them, they were certain. They believed that if they kept these laws superbly, Jehovah would disturb the Romans.

At that point the Jews would run in another, magnificent realm of Jehovah. Each great Pharisee petitioned God for that day to come. No one but Jehovah could give them their very own country and their own "Blessed One" - a Messiah-a ruler - to run them. Yet, Jehovah would not do that, they believed, until they complied with every one of the laws.

Be that as it may, there were not just the Sadducees and Pharisees in Judea. There were Essences among the Jews. They lived in towns all to themselves. They were certain that even the Pharisees didn't serve Jehovah as faithfully as they should. They, as well, searched for the Messiah. He would come when everybody became as respectful as they were, the Essenes thought.

Reach For Your Sword

The one gathering the Romans truly needed to pay special mind to was the Zealots. A Zealot loathed the Romans as much as the Pharisees and Essenes did, however he frequently attempted to take care of business. At whatever point an upset began in Judea, the Romans could be certain that there was a Zealot at its base.

Several Zealots were chased somewhere near the Romans and cold-bloodedly tormented and slaughtered.

Be that as it may, regardless of what number of were executed, there were more who might jump up in their places.

"You appeal to God for Jehovah to assist you with keeping the law and to send us the Messiah," they shouted out to the Pharisees and Essenes, "yet that isn't sufficient. Take up your swords and strike down the Sadducees and the Romans!

Simply envision somebody telling the Pharisees and Essenes that they were not doing what's necessary! In any case, the Zealots told them that. "Our dutifulness and our petitions and our swords are required," the Zealots cried. "Be prepared to strike. At that point Jehovah will send us the Messiah to lead us to triumph over the entirety of our foes."

It was no big surprise that the Romans moved rapidly to put down any such talk. Any blazing speaker or furious loyalist who went along might resemble a messiah to these Zealots. That happened ordinarily. Each time, the iron impact point of Rome squashed the Zealots into their grave.

Waiting For God

There were others in Judea, too-not Sadducees, not Pharisees, not Essenes, not Zealots. There were modest (humble) people who listened in the synagogues when the words of the Torah were read.

What's more, these expressed appreciation to God who had given his good ways to them to guide them. They listened genuinely to the words of Amos and Hosea and Isaiah-and they offered gratitude (thanks) to God who was right and loving and whose care was around them every moment of every day.

They listened in to the words of Jeremiah and Ezekiel-and they offered gratitude (thanks) to God who heard them and gave them hearts to love and obey him. They listened in to the words of the Second Isaiah-and they offered gratitude (thanks) to God who forgave their wrongdoings (sin) and helped them to serve him by serving each other. These people, as well, prayed to God for God's Messiah to come to them-to lead them in serving him and all nations.

How incredibly, unique every one of these people were. However they all met up at the Temple to worship their God.

What Happened, Herod?

Not long after the Romans took over Palestine, an Edomite named Herod became legislative leader (governor) of the Jewish people in Judea. The Jews never knew where they stood with this man. He "changed sides" at whatever point he felt like it. Herod needed to show that he was exceptionally faithful to his Roman bosses, so he constructed numerous new urban communities in the Roman design.

He set up statues of agnostic divine beings (pagan gods) and constructed sanctuaries (temples) where his people could worship the Roman emperor. Yet, he wanted to remain on the good side of the Jews, as well, so he rebuilt the Temple in Jerusalem to make it increasingly marvelous. Herod's likely idea, "My name as an extraordinary builder will stand out forever in history."

Herod was correct about this and off-base about it simultaneously. Long after the entirety of his incredible structures and urban communities had been annihilated or had gone to tidy, Herod's name would be remembered. Be that as it may, it would not be a result of anything he had done.

It would be a direct result of something that occurred in the little town of Bethlehem when he was above all else. This thing that would occur in Bethlehem was to be a higher priority than anything Herod himself at any point assembled or did.

It likewise was to be the most important thing that at any point happened to the Jews-and the most important thing that at any point happened to our world.

It was during the rule of Herod that the Old Testament reached a conclusion and the New Testament started.

Bibliography

Kaiser, W. C. (2012) Mission In The Old Testament: Israel As A Light To The Nations, 2nd Edition. Grand Rapids, MI.: Baker Academic

The Holy Bible (1964) Authorized King James Version. Chicago, Ill.: J. G. Ferguson

The Holy Bible (1982) New International Version. Grand Rapids, MI.: Thomas Nelson (Used By Permission)

The Holy Bible (1978) New York, NY.: New York International Bible Society (Used By Permission)

The Holy Bible (1953) The Revised Standard Version. Nashville, TN.: Thomas Nelson & Sons (Used By Permission)

The Holy Bible (1901) The American Standard Version. Nashville, TN.: Thomas Nelson (Used By Permission)

The Holy Bible (1959) The Berkeley Version. Grand Rapids, MI.: Zondervan (Used By Permission)

The Holy Bible (1977) The New American Standard Bible. USA.: The Lockman Foundation (Used By Permission)

The New Testament In The Language Of The People (1937, 1949) Chicago, Ill.: Charles B. Williams, Bruce Humphries, Inc, The Moody Bible Institute (Used By Permission)

The New Testament In Modern English (1958) New York, NY.: J. B. Phillips, Macmillan (Used By Permission)

The Wycliff Bible Commentary (1962, 1968) Nashville, TN.: Chicago, Ill.: The Southwestern Company, The Moody Bible Institute Of Chicago

Wiersbe, W. W. (2007) Wiersbe Bible Commentary Old Testament: The Complete Old Testament In One Volume, 2nd Edition. Eglin, Ill.: Eastbourne, UK.: David C. Cook

About The Author

THE REVEREND DR. JOHN Thomas Wylie is one who has dedicated his life to the work of God's Service, the service of others; and being a powerful witness for the Gospel of Our Lord and Savior Jesus Christ. Dr. Wylie was called into the Gospel Ministry June 1979, whereby in that same year he entered The American Baptist College of the American Baptist Theological Seminary, Nashville, Tennessee.

As a young Seminarian, he read every book available to him that would help him better his understanding of God as well as God's plan of Salvation and the Christian Faith. He made a commitment as a promising student that he would inspire others as God inspires him. He understood early in his ministry that we live in times where people question not only who God is; but whether miracles are real, whether or not man can make a change, and who the enemy is or if the enemy truly exists.

Dr. Wylie carried out his commitment to God, which has been one of excellence which led to his earning his Bachelors of Arts in Bible/Theology/ Pastoral Studies. Faithful and obedient to the call of God, he continued to matriculate in his studies earning his Masters of Ministry from Emmanuel Bible College, Nashville, Tennessee & Emmanuel Bible College, Rossville, Georgia. Still, inspired to please the Lord and do that which is well – pleasing in the Lord's sight, Dr. Wylie recently on March 2006, completed his Masters of Education degree with a concentration in Instructional Technology earned at The American Intercontinental University, Holloman Estates, Illinois. Dr. Wylie also previous to this, earned his Education Specialist Degree from Jones International University, Centennial, Colorado and his Doctorate of Theology from The Holy Trinity College and Seminary, St. Petersburg, Florida.

Dr. Wylie has served in the capacity of pastor at two congregations in Middle Tennessee and Southern Tennessee, as well as served as an Evangelistic Preacher, Teacher, Chaplain, Christian Educator, and finally a published author, writer of many great inspirational Christian Publications such as his first publication:
"Only One God: Who Is He?" – published August 2002 via formally 1ˢᵗ books library

(which is now AuthorHouse Book Publishers located in Bloomington, Indiana & Milton Keynes, United Kingdom) which caught the attention of **The Atlanta Journal Constitution Newspaper.**

Dr. Wylie is happily married to Angel G. Wylie, a retired Dekalb Elementary School teacher who loves to work with the very young children and who always encourages her husband to move forward in the Name of Jesus Christ. They have Four children, 11 grand-children and one great-grandson all of whom they are very proud. Both Dr. Wylie and Angela Wylie serve as members of the Salem Baptist Church, located in Lilburn, Georgia, where the Reverend Dr. Richard B. Haynes is Senior pastor.

Dr. Wylie has stated of his wife: "she knows the charm and beauty of sincerity, goodness, and purity through Jesus Christ. Yes, she is a Christian and realizes the true meaning of loveliness as the reflection as her life of holy living gives new meaning, hope, and purpose to that of her husband, her children, others may say of her, "Behold the handmaiden of the Lord." A Servant of Jesus Christ!

About The Book

It's anything but an upbeat thing to find that we are what's up in God's reality. This equitable carries us to another and greater inquiry. Could we ever change to become the sort of people God wants us to be? Can we come to believe God with the goal that we will obey Him?

The appropriate response of Christians to this inquiry is, "Yes!" God made us to belong to him. He doesn't abandon us. Despite the fact that over and over we choose our own specific way rather than his way, God still wants us to trust and obey him. Yet, by what means can that ever truly occur?

Now and again we wish God would make us trust and obey him. In any case, God can't do that. He would make us scared of him, but not even God can make us confide in him. That can come about only when we ourselves come to love God. Only that can make us confide in God and want to obey him.

Rather than attempting to make us love

him, God continues showing us how much he loves us. This is God's way of bringing us to love him with the goal that we will confide in him and want to obey him. The genuine story in the Bible is the account of how God has helped us to know his love for us.

This publication, "The Way Of God In The Old Testament," is about people and the things that transpired. It is about the way in which God used these people and events to help us with knowing his love for us. It is the story of God's way for saving us from being wrong, sinful and for helping us to bring about the kind of world that he meant his world to be.

This publication is the beginning of the story. At the point when you have followed the story, "The Way Of God In The Old Testament," you will see that God's Way for us goes on into the New Testament. This is a long and exciting story.

The Reverend Dr. John Thomas Wylie

Printed in the United States
By Bookmasters